WINGS AND ROCKETS

ALSO BY JEANNINE ATKINS

Mary Anning and the Sea Dragon
  with pictures by Michael Dooling
Robin's Home
  with pictures by Candace Whitman

WINGS AND ROCKETS

THE STORY OF WOMEN IN AIR AND SPACE

JEANNINE ATKINS

PICTURES BY DUŠAN PETRIČIĆ

FARRAR, STRAUS AND GIROUX   NEW YORK

Library of Congress Cataloging-in-Publication Data
Atkins, Jeannine, date.
    Wings and rockets : the story of women in air and space / Jeannine Atkins ; pictures
by Dušan Petričić.— 1st ed.
        p. cm.
    Summary: Tells the stories of women who have dared to challenge prejudices and rules
to take their place in the skies—from Katharine Wright and Bessie Coleman to Jackie
Cochran, Shannon Lucid, and Eileen Collins.
    Includes bibliographical references and index.
    ISBN 0-374-38450-9
    1. Women air pilots—Biography—Juvenile literature.   2. Women astronauts—
Biography—Juvenile literature.   3. Air pilots—Biography—Juvenile literature.
4. Astronauts—Biography—Juvenile literature.   [1. Air pilots.   2. Astronauts.
3. Women—Biography.]   I. Petričić, Dušan, ill.   II. Title.

TL539 .A85 2003
629.13'092'273—dc21
[B]
                                                        2002020022

To Bruce Carson, Dina Friedman, and Lisa Kleinholz
—J.A.

In memory of my father, Ilija,
who knew how to fly
—D.P.

CONTENTS

PART I
DREAMS AND BEGINNINGS
(1903–26)

1 KATHARINE WRIGHT

Whenever she found something broken, Katharine Wright crept past the room where her father wrote sermons to find her mother. Father was handy with words, but Mother could fix anything. She taught Katharine and her brothers how to use a hammer and a wrench; she helped them saw boards for wagons and measure runners for sleds. She didn't consider her five children properly dressed until they had string in their pockets, whether for fishing or for lengthening the line on a kite—or for solving problems no one could predict.

Katharine was the youngest, but as the only girl she was responsible for many household chores. Every Saturday morning, she dusted her father's books and Bibles. Her mother didn't complain if she stopped to look at the maps tucked between pages. Mother never scolded when Katharine went to the porch to shake dirt off a rug and came back half an hour later. She understood that the wide sky was more important than tidy floors.

Katharine was twelve when her mother fell ill with tuberculosis. Katharine now fixed meals, washed clothes and hung them to dry, and helped her oldest brothers, Reuchlin and Lorin, to plan their weddings and move from the house.

When Mother became too weak to get out of bed, Wilbur, the third brother, carried her downstairs. Katharine entertained her by talking about the Greek and Roman myths she was studying. Wilbur and the youngest brother, Orville, discussed problems with an old printing press they'd bought, and Mother asked questions that led to new ideas. The brothers said they'd like to start a printing business, and Mother said, "Why not?" Eventually her chest ached so much that it was hard for her to talk, but her eyes sparkled as Katharine described the sun god Apollo and the moon goddess Diana.

More and more often, Mother just stared out the window.

"What are you looking for?" Katharine asked.

"Promise me you'll look after your brothers when I'm gone," she replied.

Soon afterward, when Katharine was fourteen, her mother died. After the funeral, Katharine stood in their kitchen, thanking neighbors for casseroles and cookies. Didn't everyone know that it wasn't her mother's cooking she'd miss but rather her certainty that anything was possible?

Katharine stopped putting her brown hair in braids and began to pin it above her neck, the way her mother had worn her own. As soon as she got home from school, she filled the house with the sound of clattering dishes and the scent of freshly washed shirts. She followed recipes her mother had written in her bold script, fixed doors that stuck, patched broken pipes, and repaired a leak under the kitchen sink.

Katharine was determined to stay in school, though Wilbur and Orville both left high school before receiving a diploma. At first the brothers concentrated on their printing business. But once they'd figured out how to make their press run faster and smoother, they lost interest. They started buying damaged bicycles and used the good parts to build new ones. With the wind tugging their jackets, they rode as fast as horses.

Katharine tried pedaling around the barn, but her long skirt and petticoats got in the way. She'd heard of girls in cities who sometimes wore wide pants called bloomers, but that didn't seem proper for a minister's daughter.

"There must be dozens of ways to make bicycles go faster," Orville said.

"Why don't we start a bicycle repair shop?" Wilbur replied.

"Why not?" Katharine said.

The year Katharine graduated from high school, her brothers established the Wright Cycle Company. The dirt and cobblestone roads ensured that tires were always going flat, and Wilbur and Orville kept busy with repairs. They closed the shop on Sundays, but even on the Sabbath they couldn't stop thinking about motion. Wilbur, Orville, and Katharine hiked through fields, studying the shapes and movement of birds' wings. They stared at swooping hawks, noting the way they turned by tilting one wing down while raising the other.

"Imagine how fast you could go in the sky with nothing in the way," Orville said.

"Do you suppose it's possible . . ." Wilbur didn't need to finish the sentence for Orville and Katharine to know what he was thinking.

The brothers looked at Leonardo da Vinci's drawings of a man with wings. They wrote letters to other inventors. They sketched, read, and argued about the possibilities of flight. Sometimes Katharine heard Wilbur whistling upstairs, while in the kitchen Orville hummed the same song.

"If only our lives could stay like this," Orville said one morning as they joined Father at breakfast. He was the youngest of the Wright boys, distinguished by the snazzy socks that peeked beneath his gray trousers.

"Why shouldn't they?" Wilbur replied. "Just as long as none of us runs off and gets married."

"We don't have time for experiments and wives, too," Orville agreed. "Let's vow never to marry."

Wilbur shook Orville's hand, but Katharine tucked her hands in her pockets. Lately she'd spent more time staring out windows, wondering about places she'd never seen and people she'd never met. In this house she'd always be her brothers' little sister. She wanted to travel, like her father, who crisscrossed the country to organize church meetings and conferences.

"If I'm not going to marry, I don't want to depend on Father's or your money," Katharine said.

"We make enough to support all of us," Orville said. "Everything we have is yours."

"They let women into the college at Oberlin," Katharine replied. Teaching school was one of the few jobs open to an educated woman, and Katharine thought she'd like to stand in front of a chalkboard, with students looking to her for answers. "I want to learn more history, then teach it."

"History!" Wilbur cried. "What's the point of learning about discoveries that have already happened?"

"History doesn't change." Ever since Mother died, Katharine liked things to remain the same.

"With four boys, I thought at least one might follow in my footsteps and study for the ministry," Father said. "Not that I complain. All do honest work. But I'm pleased that one of my children wants to go to college."

"Who will cook for us?" Orville asked.

"We'll do it ourselves," Father said.

The next fall, Katharine boarded a train that sped across Ohio from their home in Dayton to Oberlin. She took mathematics classes, which her mother would have enjoyed, but she concentrated on Latin and Greek, as her father had. She studied the rise and fall of Rome, and she translated myths, slipping one word in place of another as she wrote about girls who turned into trees, a white bull, or a star. Some people said that she was studying too hard, but earning top grades in college seemed easier than doing all the things her mother had done.

At Oberlin, Katharine met a kind, quick-witted writer named Henry Haskell, who escorted her to picnics in the spring and sleigh rides in the winter. Although Katharine had learned to raise her hand with confidence in the classroom, when Henry whispered that her thick, brown hair was pretty, she blushed and couldn't speak. At the same time, Katharine remembered that whenever she came home on vacations, Wilbur and Orville spoke not only of their new interest in flying machines but of how tired they were of their own plain cooking—usually eggs and toast—and of how much they looked forward to her college graduation.

Shortly before graduation, Henry said that he couldn't imagine his life without her in it. Katharine started to smile. Then she thought about her brothers, and the promise to look after them. "I hope you'll visit us in Dayton," Katharine told Henry.

Katharine returned home. She missed her old beau, but she cheered up when she got a job at the high school and convinced the principal to let her start Greek and Latin classes. Even before telling her father the good news, she hired a fourteen-year-old girl named Carrie to help with the cooking and cleaning.

Soon Katharine was busy teaching, challenging students to ask why and why not. She liked writing lists of Latin verbs and reading essays, then coming home to find sketches of birds, scribbled equations, books about the weather, and Wilbur's harmonica on the kitchen table. At supper, the family often discussed other inventors' experiments with model planes propelled by twisted rubber bands, or with contraptions launched from catapults. While the Wrights were intrigued by people who rode on gliders or in balloons filled with hot air, they knew that gliders couldn't stay up for long, and it seemed impossible to steer a balloon.

Wilbur and Orville were determined to design a flying machine with a motor so it wouldn't be dependent on the whims of the wind. They constructed models from paper and cardboard and set them up attached to the string they always kept in their pockets. They studied the way the blades of a fan moved air, then designed a propeller. Katharine corrected spelling and graded tests while Orville spread cloth across the floor to measure and cut. Their mother's old sewing machine clattered and hummed as Wilbur stitched the heavy fabric into wings.

In their shop, the brothers built a plane they hoped was strong enough to carry someone, yet light enough to fly. They named it the *Flyer*. Katharine went to look at it one evening, when the dishes were done. It was somewhat bigger than a horse and carriage, its wings extending from one wall to the other. In the middle of the fragile machine was a narrow space where a person could lie down to steer by pulling rods that twisted the cloth-covered wings.

"Isn't it about time to see if it flies?" Katharine asked.

Her brothers smiled, but Wilbur said, "It won't stay up forever. It could be smashed when it lands on the rocky fields around here."

"And the neighbors will be there laughing," Orville added.

"You've got to find a quiet spot where the ground is softer," Katharine said. "What about a sandy beach?"

"With strong sea winds." Wilbur's voice sounded hopeful.

Orville got out the atlas. He drew his finger from Ohio to the North Carolina coast and said, "We should write to the weather bureau and order charts. We'd have to take apart the *Flyer* and ship it in pieces, then put it back together. By the time we tested the winds, we could be gone for months."

"We can't leave the bicycle shop that long," Wilbur said. "What will we do for money?"

Only the faint sound of crickets came through the windows.

Katharine spoke up. "My salary is enough to take care of most of our bills. I've saved some money. You can hire someone to run the shop while you're gone. I'll stop in after school's out to make sure everything is going smoothly."

Orville smiled. "What would we do without you?"

Orville and Wilbur chose a small fishing village called Kitty Hawk as their destination. In the fall of 1900, Katharine helped her brothers pack a tent, binoculars, books, glue, nails, and string, of course. Wilbur and Orville collected bicycle hubs and tire cement from the shop, along with other things that might come in handy for repairs. Before watching the train speed away, Katharine tucked in a jar of homemade jelly. She was glad to give her brothers something, but she was envious, too. She couldn't help wishing that just once someone would turn the kitchen steamy and fragrant to make something simple and sweet for her. Even more, she wished she could see the *Flyer* leave the earth.

Monday through Friday, Katharine taught her classes. Then, after the last bell, she stopped at the bicycle shop to talk with customers and check the addition and subtraction in the account books. She corrected neighbors who hinted that her brothers were wasting their time and possibly crazy. She wrote letters to Wilbur and Orville and waited for replies. Their letters were slow to arrive, but old news was better than none. The last thing Katharine wanted was a telegram, which the thrifty Wright family sent only when someone died.

Sometimes Henry Haskell took the train from Kansas City to tell Katharine about his newspaper job and ask about her life. Henry looked at her hands when they weren't holding chalk or a spoon, but were simply resting on her lap. He said that she was beautiful. Katharine longed to touch Henry's wrists, but at the door, when he moved closer, she thought of the way Orville had said, "What would we do without you?" Katharine put her hands behind her back and said good night in the same firm voice she used with students who asked for more time on an assignment.

Wilbur and Orville came home to work in the bicycle shop through most of the busy spring and summer seasons. They weren't discouraged that the flying machine hadn't gone up with one of them as pilot; they weren't even surprised. Most experiments are filled with more failures than triumphs, and every failure taught them something.

The brothers ran hundreds of tests, and when they'd improved their flying machine they returned to Kitty Hawk, in 1901. After a few months of testing their flying machine on windy North Carolina beaches, they came home to earn money and experiment with models.

In the fall of 1902, they were ready to go back to Kitty

Hawk. For the third time in three years, Katharine said good-bye and helped look after the bicycle shop. Her students kept her from getting too lonely, but sometimes, as she listened to pencils scrape in the classroom, she wondered if Wilbur was skimming through the sky or if Orville was racing toward the ocean. Could the machine have broken? Were the cloth wings drenched by waves? It was terrible not to know if her brothers were alive.

They returned home, then left again in the following fall, 1903. It was harder than ever for Katharine to convince the neighbors that her brothers weren't shiftless or deranged. She taught her students about Hermes, the Greek god with winged sandals, and Pegasus, the flying horse, but she felt she had told those tales too many times. In the evenings, she admired the babies of old school friends and longed to hold something small and precious in her arms.

Then one blustery December day a telegram arrived.

"Don't open it," Father said.

But she did. The telegram was short, but *success* was the only word she needed to read.

Katharine's cheeks burned with excitement. When Orville and Wilbur returned just before Christmas, they described how the sand blew through their hair and into Orville's striped socks and their lunches, and how they didn't mind because the sand was blown by wind that would lift them into the sky.

"We flipped a coin to see who would go up first," Orville said.

"We shook hands for good luck," Wilbur added.

"Then I flew." Orville broke into a grin as he used the word that had once belonged mostly to birds.

Those twelve seconds above the earth changed their lives. But just as every failure was a step, so was this triumph. If Wilbur and Orville could build a machine that flew, they could make it fly higher. They could make it stay in the air for minutes instead of seconds. Right after the holidays, the brothers returned to work at home.

Now that they knew what was possible, the Wrights cared less about gossiping neighbors. Katharine drove cows out of a neighbor's pasture, where her brothers tested the flying machine.

The Wright brothers spent the next few years making their invention faster, more reliable, and capable of carrying two people in a sitting position, which would make it possible for the pilot to take a passenger. They wrote letters to U.S. government officials, whose replies were skeptical. More interest came from France. Wilbur and Orville closed the bicycle shop. Wilbur boarded a ship to France to demonstrate the flying machine, while Orville went to Washington, D.C.

Katharine wondered what was the point of her promise to look after her brothers if they were going to spend so much time away from home. She had never told her brothers she wouldn't marry, but when they spoke of their perfect family arrangement, she didn't confide that she sometimes wished for something different. She was planning a visit to Kansas City when a telegram arrived.

"Don't open it," Katharine's father said.

But she did.

The plane Orville had been piloting had crashed. His pas-

senger had been killed, and Orville was badly injured. Katharine hugged her father, told Carrie to take good care of him, and rushed to the train station. Any nurse could change Orville's bandages and bring him soup, but she was the only one who would ask when he'd be back in the sky.

Katharine stayed by her brother's side for weeks, while his broken bones healed. She made sure he had clean, dapper socks, and she read aloud letters from Wilbur, who wrote of the crowd of ten thousand who came to see him fly in France.

One day Orville picked up his crutches and hobbled to the window. He said, "I've got to get back to work. I'm going to meet Wilbur in France."

Katharine looked through the window. She had never been so close to the ocean, and hadn't even had a chance to taste salt on her lips. She'd spent every day and night beside her brother. Why had her mother told her to look after her brothers, instead of telling her only daughter that there was a world out there for her to explore?

"I'm coming, too," Katharine said. "You'll need someone to catch you if you lose your balance on those crutches."

"What about your classes?" Orville asked.

"The teacher taking my place can continue through the year."

"And Father?"

"Carrie will keep on getting his meals," she said.

"He'll miss talking to you."

"People survive loneliness."

Orville gazed at his sister for a minute. Then he said, "I couldn't wish for better company."

Katharine wrote to their father, to the high school, and to Henry Haskell. She bought two tickets for a ship. On the deck, she helped steady Orville as they were knocked by strong sea winds. When another passenger remarked, "Do you suppose a plane will ever fly across the ocean?" everyone but Katharine and Orville laughed. Katharine smiled politely, knowing that anything was possible.

In Paris, Katharine admired the Eiffel Tower and the stained glass windows of Notre Dame Cathedral. She hiked past statues of Greek and Roman gods and goddesses in the Louvre Museum. She listened to the mix of languages in cafés, and she bought a hat with feathers and fancy netting. She walked down wide boulevards and narrow stone streets touched by history.

But nothing was as marvelous as the field where Wilbur stood beside his two-seated flying machine. As Katharine and her brothers talked, it seemed that they'd never been apart, that they were still at their kitchen table, instead of surrounded by curious strangers jostling to get a better view of the flying machine. Wilbur had been using the two-seated plane to teach others to pilot. He hoped the new pilots would demonstrate the planes to build interest from investors, leaving him more time to concentrate on improving the plane's design.

Wilbur introduced Katharine and Orville to Hart Berg, the business manager he'd hired, and to his wife. "Your brother gave me a ride the other day," Mrs. Berg told Katharine. "Imagine, making me the first woman to fly as a passenger in a plane."

"You won't be the last." Katharine turned to Wilbur and said, "You don't think I came this far just to look?"

"You're wearing a dress." Wilbur frowned slightly.

"What else would a lady wear?" Katharine laughed. Then she realized that her skirt and petticoats would blow in the wind and show her ankles. Her voice was firm as she said, "I don't care if I'm improper."

"A flapping skirt could push the flying machine off course," Wilbur explained.

Katharine stared. Could she have waited this long to be stopped by a foolish dress? She slipped her hands into her pockets, then smiled when she touched a familiar piece of string. She sat on the *Flyer*'s wooden seat, pressed her ankles together, and handed the string to Orville. He tied it around the bottom of her skirt.

"Aren't you afraid?" reporters asked.

Katharine didn't answer or look directly at the flying machine's thin cloth and fragile wood. She tried to forget the pictures she'd seen of the crushed and splintered plane that had left Orville with broken bones and his passenger dead. She sat with a stiff back beside Wilbur, who solemnly nodded to an assistant who spun the propellers.

The engine turned over. The bicycle chains attached to pulleys clattered. Wilbur pulled back a lever, and the flying machine rose from the ground.

Soon the wide sky was right at Katharine's feet. The earth had never been so far away, yet it had never seemed so precious. She looked down and could hardly tell men from women, rich from poor. She'd been wrong when she said that history didn't change. History was changing before her eyes. Now that she had seen the world from above, her life would never be the same.

Katharine looked straight ahead at the blue horizon and thought, *Faster. Let's go faster.* She never wanted to come down.

—

During the next few years, the Wright brothers worked to make their planes faster, safer, and able to stay in the air for longer and longer periods. Other inventors, most notably Glenn Curtiss, studied what the Wrights had done, thought of improvements, and built airplanes of their own. Few of these early machines could stay in the air for much more than thirty minutes, and many of the first pilots died when the planes crashed. Yet the practical possibilities of airplanes seemed greater than those of hot-air balloons, which previously had been the best way to see the earth from above.

Women had risen in balloons since 1804, when in France, Madame Madeline Blanchard was named the first Official Aeronaut of the Empire. Later, in England, Margaret Graham, who billed herself as "Suffragette and Showgirl," had her long gowns made to match the silk of her balloon. Once, when her balloon was punctured by a branch, her wide skirt billowed open like a parachute and softened her fall.

As women in baskets dangling beneath balloons became less thrilling to paying crowds, Dolly Shepherd grew famous for swinging from a trapeze beneath a balloon. One time the valve on her balloon stuck, and she hung on for hours, drift-

ing over meadows and villages, until the wind blew the balloon close enough to a tree for her to leap into its branches and shinny back to earth.

After the Wright brothers made their powered aircraft in 1903, people still enjoyed watching aeronauts, but more and more spectators gathered in fields to marvel as flying machines lumbered and swooped and churned overhead. Some men and women lined up to pay for a ride above the earth. They loved the way their hearts beat when they were in the air. They saw treetops and rooftops and backyards they'd never seen before.

A glimpse could make a passenger want what she'd never before thought of wanting.

In 1910, a woman demanded to be at the controls.

2 BLANCHE STUART SCOTT TAKES OFF

Blanche Stuart Scott snapped goggles over her eyes, wrapped veils around her hair, hitched her skirts up over her ankles, and climbed into an automobile. As it clattered over dirt roads, bolts and screws fell off. Blanche replaced them. Tires went flat, and she patched them. Roads appeared that weren't on her maps, and marked highways stopped in the middle of prairies. Rain leaked through her slicker and fogged her goggles. But day after day, Blanche drove across prairies and mountains and deserts.

She made it from New York to California. She shook dust off her dress and smiled for the reporters who'd gathered to take pictures of one of the first women to motor across the country. She didn't stick around to answer many questions, though, because she had a new adventure in mind.

Blanche headed to an aircraft factory run by Glenn Curtiss. "I came to learn how to fly," she said.

"Does your mother know you're here?" Glenn Curtiss replied.

"Of course. But I'm twenty-four years old and do as I please. Your advertisements say that you can teach anyone to fly."

"I never gave a girl a lesson, and I never will," Mr. Curtiss said.

"I just got a lot of publicity for Overland automobiles by driving one across the country. A woman pilot would be good for your business."

"It would ruin my business if you crashed. Everyone would blame me for letting a young lady go up."

"I don't plan to wreck the plane."

"No one plans to break his neck, but it happens."

Mr. Curtiss walked away, but Blanche stayed to watch a pilot perch on a small seat in front of the plane's engine and grab the wheel attached to a stick that rose between his knees. Blanche could see the way he pulled the stick toward him to point the plane's nose up. She squinted to watch the pilot in the sky, where he pushed the stick forward to head down. To turn right or left, he twisted the wheel in the direction he wanted to go, the way Blanche had steered her automobile.

Blanche returned to the airfield the next day and the next. At the end of the week, Mr. Curtiss said, "You're not going to leave, are you?"

"Not until I get in a plane," she replied.

Mr. Curtiss sighed, but he spent the next few days lecturing Blanche about wind currents, thrust, and the physics of flying. He guided her around the small factory, where men sawed wood frames or welded metal for propellers, and women bent over sewing machines, stitching wings. Finally, Mr. Curtiss let her pilot a plane down the runway, but he'd wired back the throttle to keep the plane from leaving the ground.

Early one morning, Blanche unblocked the throttle and sat down on the plane's small, hard seat. The engine sputtered. She opened the throttle to release more fuel to the engine, to give it more power. The canvas and wooden wings creaked as the plane rose from the ground. Blanche didn't fly high: she barely rose above the treetops. She didn't go far: she could as easily walk the length of the field. But for a minute the sky was not only overhead but all around her.

When the plane glided down, men raced toward her.

"Something must have happened to the throttle block," Blanche told Mr. Curtiss.

He opened his mouth, but before he could speak, a pilot shouted, "It's a record! Blanche Scott is the first American woman to fly!"

"It was an accident," another pilot muttered, but the news spread. Reporters arrived and snapped pictures of Blanche standing by the Curtiss planes. "Are you taking lessons?" they asked.

"Anyone can learn to fly one of my planes," Mr. Curtiss boasted. Then he murmured, "Just this once, I'll teach a girl."

Blanche flew so expertly, and she brought so much attention to the planes Glenn Curtiss sold, that he asked her to
join his exhibition team. She learned how to do loops in the
air, rising swiftly up, twisting down, then shooting up again.
She flew upside down. Since her plane didn't have a seat belt
and the cockpit was open, she held tight to the stick and
braced her feet so that she wouldn't fall out of the plane. She
flew beneath bridges, skimming rivers. She became famous
for her "Death Dive," in which she zoomed straight to the
earth, then, a few feet from the ground, swiftly steered the
plane back up. She was known as the Tomboy of the Air, and
her flying was advertised on posters as "a thrill every second."

During her first year of flying, Blanche found out that a
few women had become pilots. Bessica Raiche and her
husband had built a biplane—a plane with double-decker
wings—in their backyard out of bamboo, piano wire, and
Chinese silk. Blanche looked forward to meeting two other
women aviators at an air show in Massachusetts.

Over five thousand people crowded a field by Boston harbor, where spectators watched pilots perform stunts or leap
from planes while opening parachutes. Blanche introduced
herself to Matilde Moisant. Along with her friend Harriet
Quimby, Matilde had taken lessons from her brother. Matilde
wasn't flying that day and was dressed like many of the other
women, in a long white dress, elbow-length gloves, and a
wide-brimmed hat decorated with silk flowers.

Harriet Quimby was surrounded by a crowd of autograph-seekers. Her goggles were pushed up above her blue eyes. She wore a purple satin outfit with a hood, fitted bodice, and rippling pantaloons. Her black boots had small curved heels. Blanche realized that stuffing petticoats into wide trousers, the way she did, was hardly flattering. Since there were no outfits for women aviators, she supposed Harriet had been wise to design her own.

"Congratulations on earning a pilot's license," Blanche said to Matilde. "I've been busy, and not having a license hasn't stopped me much, but I suppose I should get one soon."

"The test isn't hard. All we had to do was steer the plane around a few pylons, then land near a big sheet placed on the ground. I got close enough, but Harriet landed right in the middle."

"I heard you got your license two weeks after Harriet got hers," Blanche said.

"Harriet hopes to make a living at flying, and being the first woman to earn a pilot's license gave her the publicity to find sponsors," Matilde said. "I made sure she took her test first."

"It was kind of you."

Matilde shrugged. "Harriet's my best friend. Anyway, she would have gotten attention. She's not the quiet type. When her first newspaper editor insisted he didn't need a lady reporter, she kept haunting his office, turning in stories so good that he agreed he might as well put her on staff."

Blanche knew Matilde wasn't shy, either. She'd heard how

Matilde became the first woman to fly in Mexico by cruising over the President's palace and dropping a bouquet weighted with a stone as a thank-you gift for dinner.

"Some people are just finding out that Harriet became the first woman to fly over the English Channel a few months ago," Blanche said. "It was hard luck that she landed a few hours after the *Titanic* sank."

Matilde nodded. "That tragic news was on the front page of every paper. Harriet's triumph was stuck in the back pages."

"She might have gotten more press if she hadn't survived. Headlines about crashes sell newspapers." Blanche smiled. It wasn't funny, but she sometimes joked about death as a way to cope with the knowledge that thirty-seven people—one of every seven pilots—had died in accidents in the past year. Even more had been hurt.

"When is Harriet scheduled to fly?" Blanche asked.

"Not till almost evening. As a finale, she's going to take the man who organized this meet for a ride in her two-seater Blériot. She's hoping to break a speed record."

"And I want to break the endurance record," Blanche said. She hoped to stay aloft through the afternoon, perhaps into the evening, and have her feat mark the amazing end of the show.

She excused herself to check her plane, making sure every wire was securely connected, every screw tight, and the gas tank properly filled. She stuffed her petticoats into her trousers, and climbed into the open cockpit. Four mechanics held back the plane, which didn't have brakes, while another pushed the propellers to set them spinning. When Blanche felt the tug of the plane was right, she took a deep breath and gave the men the thumbs-up sign. They let go. The plane clattered over the packed dirt runway, building up power. Wind rushed above her head as Blanche steered it into the sky.

Through the next few hours, Blanche kept the plane moving in wide, steady circles. She had a splendid view of Boston's Old North Church, the State House, red brick buildings, wharves, and ships at the edge of the dark blue sea. When other pilots performed stunts, Blanche flew farther out over the ocean to avoid the unpredictable air currents made by their planes.

Blanche admired the way wings wound over wings as pilots made loop-the-loops, and she did her own as gracefully as she might tie a bow. Blood rushed to her head from being briefly upside down.

By the time her gloves no longer kept her hands warm and her neck and back had gotten stiff, Blanche noticed that it was Harriet's turn. She watched Harriet and her passenger lift off in a white plane. They headed over the bay toward a lighthouse about eight miles away. When the setting sun turned the sky orange and pink, Harriet's plane made a lovely silhouette as she smoothly turned around the island and headed back.

The gold dome of the State House reflected the last of the sunlight. Blanche continued to circle the airfield while watching Harriet prepare for a landing. She saw Harriet's plane shudder, then pitch forward. The passenger was tossed from his seat, rising in a small arc before he plummeted. The sky in front of Blanche turned black for a moment. Her own plane dipped. Then she willed her mind to focus and forced strength back into her hands.

As Blanche leveled her plane, Harriet's teetered and straightened. Its nose dipped again. Its tail shot up. Harriet slipped off her seat. A purple streak briefly slashed the sky.

The pilotless plane bucked, swerved, then, caught by a gentle wind, swooped down to the shallow salt water.

Blanche steered her plane down as people raced over the runway, huddling together, pointing toward the sea. Landing was the most dangerous part of flying, since the target was a small strip of land rather than the open sky, and the hard earth was unforgiving. A sudden shift of speed, a bump, could rip a plane apart.

Blanche circled the field while a few men managed to shove most people to the edges of the runway. Still, there wasn't enough room to slow down gradually. Blanche had to land hard.

She stepped down from her plane and shouldered her way through the noisy crowd. The wheels of Harriet's white plane were sunk in the mud and water, but the plane was perfectly upright, barely harmed. Small waves lapped in and out. Men rolled up their trousers and ran through the shallow water. Doctors raced ahead with black bags and a stretcher. A reporter jogged toward the bodies without taking his pipe from his mouth. Blanche watched a boy pull out a pocket knife and slice a scrap of canvas from the plane's wing for a souvenir.

Blanche stared at the sky, then forced herself to face what

might happen to her someday. She watched a man lift Harriet Quimby so that her head dropped behind his shoulder. Her purple satin outfit was smeared with mud. Her legs dangled, and her boots with the little curved heels tapped against his knees.

Blanche knew that luck could turn as quickly as the plane that now rested in the bay. Skill and determination got a pilot up in the sky. Well-maintained equipment was necessary to keep the pilot there. But chance could bring down the greatest pilots. The wind could pick up too fast. Often, design flaws were discovered only after a plane had crashed.

Blanche found Matilde alone at the edge of the water. They listened to murmurs and cries and the hungry sound of mud pulling at shoes, trying to suck them in. They looked at the sky, which moments before had been streaked with brilliant pinks and orange. Now it was almost black.

A reporter recognized Blanche and Matilde and hurried toward them. "Miss Scott, what did the accident look like from the air? What went through your mind?" The badge tucked in the brim of his hat noted that he was with the New York World. He held a pencil poised over a little notebook.

"She was a very careful pilot," Blanche said, glancing at Matilde, whose lips trembled.

"Do you think the motor failed?" the reporter continued. "Was the two-seater too heavy? Did her passenger tip the plane? He was quite a big man."

"Did you know Matilde was Harriet's best friend?" Blanche asked, looking at the man's knuckles as he gripped his pencil. "Harriet was a reporter. Did you know her?"

"I'd heard of her." He asked again, "Can you tell me what the crash looked like from the air?"

Blanche gently took off Matilde's glasses, which had begun to fog, and wiped them.

The reporter looked impatient. "I guess you missed your chance to break the endurance record, Miss Scott."

"There will be other days to break records," she replied.

"You're going back up after what you saw?"

"Of course I am," Blanche said. She knew the sky was a country to be explored, and there were no discoveries without danger.

—

Blanche Stuart Scott spent six years traveling around the country, doing stunts in the air, but she was frustrated at being kept from learning engineering, mechanics, and more practical aspects of flying. When the United States entered World War I in 1917 and she wasn't allowed to fly as an army pilot, she ended her piloting career.

She was not the only excellent aviator kept out of the war because she was a woman. Matilde Moisant's offer to serve in France was refused, so she volunteered for the Red Cross. Ruth Law, who'd begun pilot training when she witnessed Harriet Quimby's death, went on to break altitude and distance records. Despite her accomplishments, she had to be satisfied to serve her country by performing exhibition flights to raise money for hospitals, and by dropping leaflets that urged people to buy Liberty Bonds.

Women not only were kept from fighting, but were

grounded, since most domestic flying was banned until the war was over. Neta Snook, who would later teach Amelia Earhart how to fly, spent the war inspecting aircraft engines. Katherine Stinson, the first woman to fly the U.S. mail, founded an aviation school with her mother and sister, Marjorie. The Stinson sisters were barred from volunteering as army pilots, so Katherine worked as an ambulance driver in France and England. Marjorie trained Canadian pilots who served in England, and then found a job designing aircraft.

When the war, the first in which battles were fought in the sky, was over, surplus planes, including the Curtiss JN-4, were sold relatively cheaply. The pilots who bought them were often veterans who made a living by flying around the country, giving shows and offering rides to people who'd never seen a plane before. These pilots were called barnstormers, since they often flew dangerously low over barns. They slept in fields, under the wings of their planes, before heading to the next town. Their air shows were often talked about at parties, in homes, and in shops such as the one where Bessie Coleman worked.

Elizabeth "Bessie" Coleman worked in a Chicago barbershop, giving manicures to men who wanted smooth hands to show that they worked behind desks instead of in cotton fields. Bessie and her customers often talked about where they'd come from. They spoke in hushed voices of people down South who'd been killed just for stepping through the wrong door or crossing the wrong street.

But Bessie made sure that their conversations finished on a high note. Organizations such as the NAACP were being formed to protest lynchings. World War I, which people called the war to end all wars, was over. In 1920, women's struggle to obtain the right to vote had just been won. Besides, hope was a habit Bessie had learned from her mother. When her mother spoke about what her parents had endured as slaves, she always ended with tales of Harriet Tubman, who'd kept her eyes on a star as she led people north to freedom.

Bessie used to dream that she, too, would do something no one had done before. Trimming and filing nails wasn't going to make her a hero, but at least the job paid better than picking cotton or washing clothes, work she'd done back in Waxahachie, Texas. Rubbing aches from hands was one way to make life a little finer, as her mother had done by planting roses outside their crowded cabin. Things hadn't been easy for the Coleman family, but Bessie had learned that cast-off clothing could be mended and a bright cloth could cover a plain table. She'd grown up believing that life could always get better, which was the message that attracted her to the *Chicago Defender.*

Bessie was thrilled when the newspaper's respected editor came to her shop. Robert Abbott traveled around Chicago with an eye and ear out for news. He escorted Bessie to clubs where women in spangled dresses sang jazz and the blues. Bessie's high heels clicked as she danced. Robert and Bessie listened to saxophones and trombones, and talked about the poets and painters who were creating a renaissance in Harlem. Robert spoke enthusiastically about France, where many black artists and musicians were finding welcoming audiences.

Some white people came to these nightclubs. At first Bessie felt awkward, since she'd always lived in black neigh-

borhoods, gone to black schools and churches, and sat in seg-
regated cars of trains. Sometimes Robert took her to places
where they were almost the only people of color. They went
to the theater and city hall, and one day to an air show at the
local fairground.

There, Bessie watched the biplanes race toward the
ground, then pull up at the last second. One pilot flew his
plane upside down. Another wound through the sky, leaving
trails of smoke that formed the name of a hotel.

"These Curtiss Jennies were used during the war," Robert
said. "They've been bought by army pilots who don't want to
stop flying."

Bessie breathed in the scent of burnt fuel, sharp as the
smell of nail polish. When the planes made elegant loops and
zigzags, she was filled with longing. She wanted to do more
than stand and look. She wanted to do something that none
of her family or friends had ever done, except in dreams or
stories.

"Come on," Bessie said, pulling Robert through the
crowd. She strode to a tent where a white man advertised flying lessons. He tried to ignore her, but when she insisted she
wanted a lesson, he said, "You need a license."

"How do I get a license?" she asked.

"You have to take lessons."

"I want to sign up for a class," Bessie said.

"You can't, miss." The young man twisted his freckled fingers together and looked around. A woman in a hat that
shaded her pale face, a veteran leaning on crutches, and some
other people gathered to listen.

"Let's go, Bessie." Robert's voice was stern and cool. Writing for his newspaper, he was used to turning his anger into words.

"Why can't I take lessons?" Bessie said, keeping her eyes on the young man behind the table. "I have the money."

"I'm sorry," he replied.

"He's a busy man." Robert's voice turned slightly sarcastic as he tugged on her arm.

Bessie let Robert lead her away. She thought about how she hadn't been shut out of as many places as her mother had. She had gone to school, though there had been only one room and one teacher for eight grades. Lessons had stopped whenever there was cotton to be picked. She had gone to college, but when she used up the money she'd saved, no one had tried to stop her from leaving. No one had even said it was a shame.

"I will fly," Bessie told Robert. Her patience had run out. She'd picked too much cotton, done too much laundry, and manicured too many hands. She vowed to show that young man he was wrong.

During the following weeks, Bessie spoke to dozens of people and discovered that there were flying schools in New York and North Carolina, in Massachusetts and California. But no instructor had ever accepted a black student. One said he'd have to be crazy to let a black girl take the controls of a plane he was in.

"It's probably for the best. It's a dangerous sport," Robert said, trying to console her. "Those planes weren't worth much even during the war, and they're worse now. They've been fixed with wood from old crates or barrels. They're held together with gum or rubber bands and any old thing the mechanics find lying around barns. Pilots have short lives."

"At least my life would be in my own hands." Bessie's voice was clear and firm. "If there's no one in the United States who will give me lessons, I'll go somewhere else. You've always said the French make less fuss about the color of people's skin. With an international license, I could fly anywhere in the world."

"Bessie, you don't even speak French."

"I can learn," she replied.

"Traveling by train and ship will cost a lot."

"I'll save my money. I'll get a second job."

"There's nothing to say for certain that you can get a license overseas."

Bessie took a breath and pushed that thought aside. "You don't believe I can do it."

"Bessie, I think you can do anything, but—" Robert began, before Bessie interrupted.

"Who gave you permission to write the things you do?" she asked. "Did you sit and wait for someone to suggest you start your own newspaper?"

Robert looked at her for a minute. Then he said, "I could speak to some friends who might want to sponsor a very determined woman."

Bessie grabbed his hands. "I can learn to fly. I know I can."

"A black female aviator. That news could sell a lot of papers."

Bessie found another job managing a chili restaurant. She

saved her money, planned, and dreamed. A few people encouraged her, but most said that she must be some kind of
fool. Bessie didn't listen.

After working for several years, she boarded a ship to
France. In a field not far from Paris, she approached a hangar
where a man was writing in a ledger book. She said, "I came
for flying lessons."

The man looked up from the rows of numbers, but he
didn't speak.

"I want to learn to fly," Bessie said. *"Je veux apprendre à
voler."*

"Are you from England or America?" the man asked in
English.

"America," she said.

"You've come all this way for lessons?"

"Yes," Bessie said.

"Very good, *mademoiselle. Très bon.* Tomorrow at nine
o'clock. Is that a good time?"

Bessie thought she could never be happier. But she was,
the next day, in the sky.

There she watched her instructor carefully. She copied what
he did, steering with her hand on the stick, pushing or lifting
her feet on the rudder bar to move the plane up or down.

Finally, it was time to solo. As she sat in the open cockpit,
she was afraid, but she let fear be a companion. The wind whis-
tled over her head and carried away the sound of her laughter.

Courage was like a muscle that got stronger as she used it.
Bessie enjoyed perfecting her skills while traveling around Europe. After a year of flying, she returned home with a license

from the Fédération Aéronautique Internationale. She could fly anywhere on earth. But could she make a living as a pilot?

Once Bessie's ship had docked, late in the summer of 1922, Robert Abbott called some friends, who arranged for her to appear at a parade honoring the World War I veterans of New York's all-black infantry. People cheered as the soldiers marched to a field. And a band raised trombones and beat drums while Bessie Coleman strode toward a plane. She wore a belt around her slender waist, with a strap crossing her chest. Her dark eyes shone beneath the goggles she'd pushed to the top of her head.

When she stepped into the cockpit, the band played "The Star-Spangled Banner." Bessie flew over and around the field, climbing, diving, turning the plane in circles, then in figure eights. She made loops, as if she were dragging invisible banners through the sky. She never wanted to come down.

The next day, newspapers raved about the show. Word of Bessie's nerve and skill spread. Soon she was invited to perform at fields, then at bigger airstrips, in towns and later in cities. Tickets sold quickly.

Bessie earned enough money to buy her own plane. She crossed the country to California, then flew back to Chicago and finally to Waxahachie, Texas, the town where she'd grown up.

There a crowd gathered to watch her pilot her airplane toward the clouds. She stopped the plane in midair, turned it around, and sped toward the ground. Spectators ducked as she came close enough to blow off their hats. Then Bessie steered the plane back up.

A few minutes later, Bessie landed smoothly. She took off
her helmet, goggles, and gloves. People cheered. Just as Harriet Tubman had once inspired her, now Bessie showed children possibilities they'd never considered.

Girls and boys cheered and asked for autographs. "You
can do this, too," Bessie told them, and a new dream rose
within her. She wanted to open the sky to others, to make a
place where people heard "Try" and "Go on," instead of
"Stop" or "Turn back." Bessie Coleman wanted to make the
earth feel as free and splendid as the sky. She vowed to save
her money to start a school for black pilots.

"Do it again," a girl begged.

Bessie grinned as she climbed back into the cockpit. Oh
yes, she would.

—

*Sturdier, safer planes were built every year, but through
the 1920s, every plane was an experiment, and the only way
to know how fast and high it could fly was for a pilot to take
it up. Even when a plane wasn't being pushed to its limit,
things went wrong.*

*In 1926, Bessie Coleman was flying over an airfield when
her airplane flipped over, spun, and plummeted. Bystanders
first thought it was a stunt, but their gasps turned to screams
when a body spilled from the plane.*

*A wrench had been left on the floor of the cockpit. When
the plane turned to circle the field, the tool must have skidded. It jammed the motor, which ground to a halt in midair.*

Thousands came to Chicago for Bessie Coleman's funeral.

Now it would be years before her dream of a school for African American pilots would come to pass. But Bessie's flying had made more people consider a life in the sky. Women and people of color demanded jobs they'd never held before.

The world was changing. Planes were being made to fly greater distances. During the 1920s, planes regularly sank in the Atlantic Ocean as pilots tried to fly from one continent to another. When Charles Lindbergh flew from New York to Paris in 1927, the first person to fly across the Atlantic solo, he became one of the most famous people in the world.

Amy Guest, a wealthy American woman who had settled in England, bought a plane she named the Friendship, *since she hoped to fly in it between her two beloved countries. Mrs. Guest's family dissuaded her from making the dangerous trip, but she asked George Putnam, a publisher who specialized in books about adventures, to find a woman willing to ride in her place. George Putnam selected a woman who'd worked taking photographs, sorting mail, driving a gravel truck, and caring for hospitalized veterans before becoming a social worker. Some of the other women who'd been considered had more experience in cockpits, but Amelia Earhart would be a passenger, even though she was a licensed pilot. She had a modest way of speaking, like Charles Lindbergh's, and she even looked a bit like the lanky, sandy-haired man with the shy grin.*

In the spring of 1928, Amelia Earhart wrote farewell letters to be given to her mother and father if the Friendship *fell into the sea. Then she started on the trip that would change her life.*

PART II
THE FIRST WOMEN'S CROSS-COUNTRY AIR RACE
(1929)

Amelia Earhart sprawled on the *Friendship*'s floor, snapping pictures of clouds drifting above the Atlantic Ocean. She knew that whales, sharks, and schools of brilliant fish must be swimming in the cold water. No doubt they swam around some of the nineteen planes that had attempted the journey between America and Europe the year before.

But it wouldn't do much good to think about that, or about the gauge meant to pinpoint their location—it was broken. When Amelia, Wilmer "Bill" Stutz, the pilot, and the mechanic, Louis "Slim" Gordon, had been in the air all night and most of the day, their radio broke, too. Amelia knew that if they kept heading east, they'd eventually fly over Ireland, England, or France.

Then they began to run out of fuel. When they had only enough gasoline to keep them in the air for about an hour, Amelia spotted a ship. She scribbled a note asking the sailors to point out the direction of the nearest coastline, tied the note to an orange, and tossed it down to the deck. She missed. The orange sank into the sea, and the men on deck cheerfully waved.

There was nothing to do but wave back and keep going. Slim Gordon nervously nibbled at a sandwich. Finally, Amelia saw a dark shape loom in the mist. At the sight of land, Slim gleefully tossed his half-eaten sandwich out the window.

Bill Stutz guided the *Friendship* onto the water off the coast of Wales. Unaware of the length of their journey, fishermen greeted them casually.

The aviators continued to London, where they were met by cheering crowds. "How does it feel to be the first woman to fly across the Atlantic?" one reporter asked.

"The credit goes to the pilot and mechanic," Amelia said, pushing Bill Stutz and Slim Gordon toward the cameras.

But the photographers snapped pictures of Amelia. They commented on her tousled reddish-brown hair and tall, slim frame, saying, "You could be Charles Lindbergh's sister!"

"What was it like to spend twenty hours and forty minutes in the air?" one asked.

"I loved every minute," she said.

"Miss Earhart, would you do it again?"

"Yes." And next time, she vowed, she wouldn't fly as a

passenger. The next time she flew over the ocean, she would be at the controls.

After the first interviews, Amelia got some rest, then traded her beige sweater, white shirt, breeches, and boots for borrowed gowns and high heels. She attended dinner parties and dances held in her honor, before sailing back to the United States, where mayors from thirty-two cities had invited her to visit.

She quit her job as a social worker, though she'd enjoyed helping immigrant children learn English. It was hard to go back to a small room after being part of the sky. She wrote a book about her flight called *20 Hrs. 40 Mins.*, which George Putnam published that same year, 1928. She took a job doing publicity for a new commercial airline that was beginning to take passengers across the country. The rides were so bumpy that the floors were covered with rubber mats, which were easy to mop when passengers got sick. Jokes were made that TAT stood not for Transcontinental Air Transport but for "Take a Train." Amelia's job was to help convince people that these flights were comfortable and safe.

Amelia would rather fly than talk, but every time she spoke, more young women applied for pilots' licenses. She hoped that commercial airlines would open more jobs to women in plane factories and cockpits. She tried to make sure that women didn't end up serving tea on the planes' little wicker tables.

Amelia earned enough money to buy a red Lockheed Vega. After visiting her mother and sister in Massachusetts, she flew to see her father in California. This made her the first woman to fly across the country by herself, but she wanted to make the trip more quickly. She applied to take part in the most important cross-country race, which would begin in California and end in Ohio, as it had for the past few years.

The race manager said, "Miss Earhart, I'm sorry, but we're returning your application."

"Don't I have enough experience?" Amelia asked.

"Of course you do! You musn't take it personally, but this race is for men only."

"Why?"

"Miss Earhart, the pilots will be flying across mountains and deserts. If a plane breaks down, and the pilot survives the crash, there's often no place to call for help. Excuse me for being blunt, but men have died during these races."

"Like every pilot, I'm prepared to take a chance."

"But the public isn't ready! If a woman died in our race, there would be an outcry."

"Why shouldn't women take the same risks men take?"

"Miss Earhart, we know you could handle the pressure, but if we let you enter, other ladies might insist on racing, too. We could end up with a lot of blood on our hands. Men have always fought in the wars and led expeditions and captained ships. People are more used to men risking their lives."

"Plenty of women crossed the country in covered wagons. There were women aboard most ships, and if none were captains, that was only because men wouldn't let them touch the sails and wheels." Amelia argued more, but she was not allowed to enter the race.

Later, she confided her anger to Louise Thaden, a young woman who had broken women's international flight records for speed, altitude, and endurance.

"I don't think the race committee cares as much about a woman dying as about being blamed," Amelia said.

"They're always afraid of something." Louise's red hair bounced as she shook her head. "When I applied for my transport license, the tester said he'd be harder on me than on a man. He said that if I ever cracked up a plane, people would criticize him for letting a woman fly." She added, "I tried to enter the cross-country race, too."

"What did they say?"

"No. And that if they let me enter, other women might demand to race, too."

"Then he gave you the line about blood on his hands?"

Louise nodded.

"These men need to see us all together so they'll realize how many excellent women pilots there are," Amelia said.

"How do we show them if they won't let us in their race?"

"We'll hold our own race," Amelia said.

She spread the word, and in mid-August 1929, twenty women met on the California coast to begin the eight-day race to Cleveland. One journalist dubbed the race the "Powder-Puff Derby," and newspapers were filled with stories about the "flying flappers" or "sweethearts of the air." Amelia was impatient with the names—she could hardly wait for the day when women would simply be called pilots.

Amelia was happy to meet the other pilots, such as Phoebe Omlie and Blanche Noyes, who performed stunts in

planes. Flying was expensive, so many of the pilots were wealthy, including the glamorous silent screen star Ruth Elder and the socialite Opal Kunz, who'd traveled around the world with her husband on his job finding jewels for Tiffany's. Other women, such as Bobbi Trout, who ran a gas station, worked hard to buy enough flying time to set a record such as becoming the first woman to fly all night. Gladys O'Donnell and her husband had started a flying school. Margaret Perry managed a small airport. Claire Fahy and Pancho Barnes worked as test pilots. Ruth Nichols was probably the best-known aviator. She'd worked full-time as a pilot since graduating from Wellesley College seven years before. For her job demonstrating planes, she'd flown into forty-six states during the past year.

On August 18, 1929, over ten thousand people came to the Santa Monica airfield to watch the pilots take off. Ladies in fancy hats and dresses stared at the women wearing trousers, leather helmets, and goggles. Even over the roar of engines, Amelia could hear people chant, "Amelia! Amelia! Let's hear it for Lady Lindy!"

Settling into her cockpit, she licked her dry lips and checked the gauges on the control board. She tugged the straps of her parachute to make sure they were secure. She watched as mechanics cranked propellers and yanked away blocks that had been set in front of wheels.

A race official waved a red-and-white flag once every sixty seconds to signal the next pilot to take off. Amelia saw Louise Thaden's blue-and-gold plane roll down the runway and soar into the sky. Then Pancho Barnes took off. Every day the pilots' starting and landing times would be recorded, and the hours, minutes, and seconds spent in the air would be added up. The pilots would fly most of the day but stop at night, when it would be too dark to read the maps strapped to their legs so they wouldn't blow out, or to see the landmarks below. The pilot with the shortest flying time when she reached Cleveland, eight days later, would win $2,500 and a trophy.

As the starting flag was waved again, Amelia lifted her foot from the brake pedals. Her plane clattered over the runway, skimmed the ground, and rose into the sky.

Amelia glanced in the rearview mirror. Smoke a shade too dark puffed from the exhaust pipe. She checked the control panel and realized that the electric motor switch had broken. She kept flying over the trees, thinking of how she'd flown with faulty parts before. She looked ahead at the mountains, where there would be no flat places to land in an emergency. No one had radios to signal where they were, so it could be days before someone who crashed was found. The gallon of water, can of tomato juice, and malted milk tablets she'd packed wouldn't last long.

The smoke trailing behind her plane looked thicker.

Amelia turned the plane around. While the other pilots continued to take off and soar over the fields made dark by thousands of spectators and their automobiles, Amelia flew in circles. She flew down when the runway was clear.

Mechanics and reporters rushed toward her.

"Can you put in a new switch?" she asked.

One mechanic raced to the hangar for a replacement, while two others swiftly removed screws and faulty wires.

While they worked, Amelia told the reporters, "It's a minor problem."

"This won't make you lose the race?"

"Of course not," she said, though she glanced anxiously at the mechanics to see if they were almost finished. "This is only the first and shortest lap today. A lot can happen over the course of a week."

Seeing that the repairs were almost done, Amelia swung her leg up, ready to climb back into the cockpit.

"We need to run a test on this, Miss Earhart," someone said.

"I don't have time," she replied, and buckled her seat belt. She glanced at her watch. She'd lost fourteen minutes. That would put her behind today, but it needn't cost her the race. She just hoped this would be her last bit of bad luck.

Amelia steered away from the Pacific Ocean and flew over grand Hollywood homes, blue swimming pools, and movie lots nestled against hills. She checked the gauges before opening the throttle. Alert to every twist of the wind, she headed toward the mountains. She passed one plane and spotted another to the north. She increased her speed still more, though when clouds rose before her, she slowed down. It could be deadly to encounter a rocky peak at high speed.

She kept a moderate pace and before long spotted "San Bernardino," the first stop, freshly painted on the roof of a barn. Clouds of dust billowed from the airport, making it hard to see the boundaries of the landing strip.

Amelia didn't want to add minutes to her time by hovering until the air cleared. She lowered the plane without slowing much, so the wheels hit the ground with a thud. The heavy plane bounced. Then she slammed on the brakes as the plane rolled down the packed-dirt runway. She managed to cut the switch and lock the brakes when the plane was just a few feet away from the spectators. They cheered as if her sudden stop had been part of the show.

Amelia climbed out of the cockpit.

"Lady Lindy! The queen of the air!" people shouted, waving scraps of paper and tickets for her to autograph. Reporters, who knew photos of the brave and pretty woman who'd crossed the Atlantic sold a lot of newspapers, snapped pictures. "How was your ride?" they asked.

"Great!" Amelia grinned, though George Putnam had coached her to smile with her lips closed to hide the little gap between her front teeth. She looked at the pilots, who had gathered around the planes and were cleaning windshields, bending over maps, and talking.

"Did you meet Jessie Miller?" Amelia asked the reporters. "You know she's the first woman to fly from England to Australia." Then she pointed to a woman who was smoking a cigar and said, "Pancho Barnes does stunt work for the movies."

The reporters glanced at the other women, but turned back to Amelia.

Amelia lifted up some children to give them a look at her cockpit. She nudged back a lady who was poking her parasol onto the canvas wing of a plane. Then Amelia excused herself and joined Louise Thaden and another pilot.

"Did you meet Marvel Crosson?" Louise asked. "Another gal from Kansas, though she flies in Alaska now."

Amelia shook the hand of a small woman whose round face was framed with short, curly hair.

"Did you hear Louise came in first?" Marvel asked. "Pretty impressive, considering she flew with her nose pressed to a pipe she had to breathe into."

"When I flew in yesterday, I got dizzy," Louise said. "The mechanics found that carbon monoxide was going into the cockpit. They didn't have time to take everything apart, but they put in a pipe to funnel in fresh air."

"I guess I can't complain because my engine is overheating," Marvel said.

"It can't be too serious. You came in second," Louise said, before smiling to greet a woman with violet-black eyes. "Amelia, have you met Ruth Nichols?"

Amelia put out her hand, which Ruth ignored.

"That was some landing, Lady Lindy," she said.

"We've all made some rough landings," Louise said.

"It wasn't my best," Amelia admitted. "It was hard to see with all the dust."

"The dust was stirred up by all the planes that had already landed," Ruth said. "Almost everyone else was here. I thought the First Lady of the Sky forgot her directions, but of course you wouldn't do that. Didn't you do a bit of navigating while you hitched a ride over the Atlantic?"

Amelia shrugged. "I was about as useful as a sack of potatoes."

"It took guts just to set out on a trip that people said was impossible," Louise said.

"I guess it took some courage. And being friendly with George Putnam." Ruth lifted her eyebrows. She was almost the opposite of Amelia in appearance. While Amelia's hair was light, short, and straight, Ruth's hair was nearly black, long, and wavy. Amelia was tall and thin; Ruth was shorter and had a curvy figure.

"I met him when he called me for an interview," Amelia said.

"The gossip is that you and George Putnam are very close friends. Can we expect a wedding?"

"Mr. Putnam published the book I wrote about the trip." Amelia felt herself blushing. She wasn't about to confide in this woman that George had proposed more than once. "He'll make money on it, and so will I. Enough to buy a plane."

"My plane is borrowed," Ruth said.

"You're just jealous," Marvel said.

"Of flying across the ocean?" Ruth said. "Of course I am. But there's still a record waiting to be set for the first woman to pilot a plane across the Atlantic."

"And there's still this race to win." Amelia looked straight into Ruth's violet-black eyes, then turned toward the crowd, which had been shouting her name. What would they think if she didn't place well in this race? Fame came and went as fast as the wind.

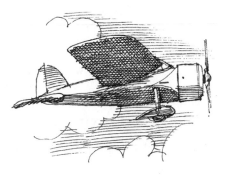

The morning sky grew lighter. Amelia dressed, twisted a scarf around her neck, and slipped on her lucky bracelet, a narrow elephant-hide band studded with tiny silver clouds. She went downstairs to a room that smelled of cinnamon and leather jackets, where she said a few friendly words to almost everyone but Ruth Nichols. Margaret Perry looked strangely flushed, but she said it was sunburn and not a fever. Opal Kunz's emerald and ruby rings sparkled as she sipped tea.

Amelia and the other pilots pulled on goggles and gloves and climbed into their cockpits. Their starting times were recorded as they headed into the sky. Amelia had gotten only a few hours of sleep, but her gaze was sharp as she focused on the horizon. She opened the throttle to the point at which she would go fast without straining the engine. Like the other pilots, she would fly during most of the daylight hours, stopping to refuel and then again for lunch.

Before long, the other planes were so far behind that she couldn't see them. For hours, Amelia flew over mountains and between hills. No painter could notice more precisely the sky's subtle alterations of color, though Amelia wasn't looking for beauty so much as for signs of storms or shifts in heat that could change the wind. When she saw white and yellow sand spread over flat land, she knew she'd almost reached Arizona. She searched for the desert airport, where the pilots were scheduled to stop for gas.

Above Yuma, she steered the plane toward the runway, leaving plenty of room to slow down gradually this time. As her plane's wheels touched the packed-dirt runway, she pressed the brakes. Windblown sand pelted the windshield. The plane skidded, and she realized she'd flown in too fast for the low resistance of thin desert air. She hadn't prepared for sand blowing around her wheels. Her plane stopped so suddenly that its nose slammed into the ground.

Amelia's forehead smacked the control board. She heard a thud and a cracking noise from the front of her plane. She unfastened her seat belt while someone asked, "Are you all right?"

"How's the plane?" Amelia struggled out without waiting for an answer. She raced to the front, where the plane's nose was half-buried in sand. The propeller had split.

"Can it be fixed?" she asked a man who'd just run over.

"Miss Earhart, I'm manager of this airfield. We've called a doctor. He's on his way."

"I'm fine," Amelia said. She pulled off her leather helmet and tried to ignore her aching head. "How long will it take to get this plane back up?"

"That propeller would take days to fix, but there's an airplane factory not far from here. We can call and see if they have extra propellers."

"Call them now!" Amelia said, then asked the mechanics, "How quickly can you get that off?"

The men righted the plane and hurried to remove the broken propeller.

"Please, no pictures," Amelia begged a reporter, who turned his camera from the damaged plane to her.

"Do you have a comment for the *World* on surviving a crash?" he asked. "Will this mean the end of racing for you, Lady Lindy?"

A mechanic was dashing across the sand, which shimmered in the hot sunlight. "They've got some propellers that should fit!" he shouted. "They'll be here soon."

"Miss Earhart, the doctor's here," the manager said.

"Thank you for coming, but I feel fine." Amelia shook the doctor's hand, then turned to drink some water and look up as a plane landed away from the worst of the sand. "Has anyone else arrived?" she asked.

"Ruth Nichols has come and flown ahead."

Amelia watched two more pilots land, refuel, and take off again before a plane arrived with the new propeller. While the mechanics started to put it on, Marvel Crosson flew down.

Amelia crossed the sand, dotted with sage and mesquite, and watched a mechanic fill Marvel's tank with gasoline while another inspected her engine.

"What happened?" Marvel nodded at Amelia's plane.

"I landed in a sand trap, but only the propeller was wrecked. I should be up again within the hour."

"They should have flagged off that area," Marvel said.

"How's your engine?" Amelia asked.

"It still seems a bit too hot. Just to be safe, the manager called Phoenix, where I'll have a new one put in tonight."

"Phoenix is halfway across the state."

"I'll let it cool down for a while." Marvel's voice was soft but firm.

"I suppose everything here seems hot after Alaska," Amelia said. "What led you up north?"

"The long light in summer is perfect for flying," Marvel said. "There aren't many railroads or roads, so most people at the outposts don't care whether it's a man or a woman who brings them food and medicine."

"I guess getting any pilot is better than waiting weeks for a dogsled."

"Yes, though there are a few who complain. One sick fellow refused to get in the plane I was piloting, even though it was his only chance to reach a doctor. He asked my brother how he could ride in a plane with a woman at the controls. Joe answered by climbing into my plane with me, flying up, then, once we were high, crawling out to walk across the wings."

Amelia grinned and turned back to her Lockheed Vega.

"It looks like the propeller's almost on. Are you sure your plane will be all right?"

"I'll take it easy." Marvel shrugged, then added, "I can't stop."

Amelia shook Marvel's small, strong hand, then crossed the field to her own plane. She asked a mechanic, "Is it ready?"

"Miss Earhart, that was some pounding your plane took. We can't let you go back up without inspecting it for hidden damage."

"I wouldn't be here if I didn't take chances. None of us would." She rubbed her sore, swollen forehead and thought of the way Margaret Perry had started out that morning, ignoring what Amelia was sure was illness. Marvel was pressing ahead despite an overheating engine.

Amelia climbed into the cockpit as the last screw was tightened.

The wind grew so strong that it took most of her strength to hold the plane steady. There were few signs of life, no houses, rivers, or railroads to guide her over long stretches of sand and treeless mountains. She kept a close eye on the fluctuations of the compass. If she shifted direction even a little too far north or south, she could be lost long before a landmark made her realize that she was off course. If she ran out of fuel but managed to land safely in the desert, she'd have to wait hours before anyone realized she was gone. She might have to wait days before she was found.

But she loved the big sky that seemed to be all hers. Finally, amid the pale rocks and sand, a spot of green glimmered in the dry heat. The desert air was so clear that she could see Phoenix almost two hundred miles away. The city grew brighter and bigger as she swept down in a smooth landing.

Amelia shrugged off reporters' questions about her crackup in Yuma and spoke of the six days of racing still ahead. After a few hours, when the pilots were escorted into town for dinner, three were still missing.

"They'll turn up," Ruth Nichols said, sitting down to a plate of chicken and potatoes.

"Bobbi is tough, and Marvel took care of herself in the wilds of Alaska, but I think Opal is more used to society balls," Louise said.

"Opal's probably talking the ear off some gold miner, making a good connection for her jeweler husband," Amelia said. "Anyway, they're sending search parties into the desert as a precaution."

Amelia wasn't worried, but she felt some tension about the missing women. By unspoken agreement, everyone had stopped speaking about them when dessert arrived.

"Why pound cake? Don't they know pilots need chocolate?" Ruth said. "The first thing I'm going to do after picking up my trophy in Cleveland is find a hot fudge sundae."

Everyone turned as a reporter came over to announce that he'd heard from Bobbi Trout, who'd flown too far south and landed in Mexico. She'd be back up and in the race as soon as it was light tomorrow.

Amelia and Louise went to the room they'd be sharing for the night. Amelia switched on a fan as Louise set a small picture on the table between the beds.

"There's nothing like spending the day in the sky," Louise said. "I've dreamed of this since I was a girl. When I was seven, I jumped off the barn roof with an umbrella over my head. I got a bit wiser a few years later, and rigged up a hot-air balloon."

"I liked riding horses, fast, and sledding," Amelia said. She pointed at the picture and asked, "Is that your husband?"

Louise nodded. "He started flying back in the war. Now he designs and builds planes. We hope to start our own airplane company someday."

"I thought you were going to say you were starting a family."

"Of course we want children, too. Don't you?"

"Babies are cute, but a child would keep me out of the sky for too long. Louise, I don't even have time for a man in my life."

"Some of the girls say that you and George Putnam are dating."

"He does publicity for me."

"That doesn't mean he can't be a beau, too."

Amelia shook her head. George was a handsome, intelligent man with a sense of adventure, but she simply didn't know anyone for whom marriage had brought the happiness that flying gave her.

She glanced at the clock and saw it was almost midnight. She was about to turn off the light when she heard voices in the hall. Amelia rushed to the door. Opal Kunz was sur-rounded by smiling pilots wearing nightgowns or long shirts. Opal's face was sunburned and smudged, except for two pale circles around her eyes where her goggles had been. Her hair was tangled, but her bracelets gleamed.

"I got lost and ran out of gas and had to come down in the desert," she said. "I managed to hike into a town where I found a few nice fellows who helped me lug some gas cans back to my plane. I guess I'm the last one to arrive."

"Marvel's not here yet," Amelia said.

"The gal from Alaska? She'll be fine," Opal assured her.

Amelia and the others went to bed, though no one seemed to sleep much. Everyone got up before dawn, climbed into her plane, and headed east over deserts and craggy mountains. Amelia was glad to be in the sky, where she couldn't think about the few hours she'd lost the day before, or about Marvel Crosson, or about anything except what was right before her eyes.

She was the first to arrive at their refueling stop. Then she, Ruth, Louise, and Pancho landed at almost the same time in El Paso, Texas, for the night.

They chatted with reporters and watched the rest of the women fly in. Amelia joined some of them in an inn where cots were squeezed between beds. They began getting ready to head for a dinner put on by a local women's club.

"I'd rather sleep outside than in here," Gladys O'Donnell said. "The fans only blow around this one-hundred-degree air."

"Jessie always wants to sleep in her plane," Pancho said.

"It has an open cockpit. You'd keep an eye on your plane, too, if you'd ever been flying with a rattlesnake that woke up from its nap," Jessie Miller said. "I had to break off the stick to club the thing, then fly the plane upside down to make it fall out."

Amelia fastened her silk stockings. She was starting to put on her shoes when she heard a sob and a scream coming from downstairs.

Her hand froze on the heel. She had the wild hope that if she kept her hand still, nothing in the world would change. But she slipped on both shoes and ran downstairs.

There, Louise had her arm around Gladys, who was crying. Margaret Perry's face was red. Three men looked at the floor.

"Apparently, the motor failed," a reporter said. "By the time Marvel gave up on the plane and jumped, she was too close to the ground for her parachute to open."

Amelia made her face stiff as she wondered if Marvel had heard the motor grind louder, then become strangely quiet. Did she wrestle with the wind, trying to keep the plane from spinning? She must have done everything she could to save the plane before she threw her legs over the edge, jumped, and pulled the parachute's rip cord as the hard earth loomed.

"The news is being wired around the country," the reporter said. "People are saying this accident proves that women can't fly. Sponsors are threatening to withdraw."

"The race is going to be canceled," another reporter said.

"No," Louise said.

Ruth spoke up. "Pilots have died during the men's races."

Amelia looked at the other women. They all understood that no one had the right to keep a pilot from the sky.

"Has someone notified Marvel's brother?" she asked.

The reporters shrugged.

"He's in Alaska," Amelia said. "It may take a few days to find him. We'll have time to finish this race, then get back to California for the funeral."

"You're not saying you'll go on with the race!" the reporter exclaimed.

"I won't stop." Amelia repeated what might have been Marvel's last words.

"I never really spoke with Marvel," Ruth said softly. "I didn't even know she had a brother."

"He used to walk across the wings of her plane," Amelia said, imagining Marvel's small, strong hands on the controls, her eyes sparkling as she claimed a place in the cold, northern skies.

At three o'clock in the morning, Amelia stopped tossing in her bed. She dressed, switched off the fan, tiptoed through the dark, hot building, and went outside. Louise and half the other pilots were checking their planes' engines, wiring, and fuel levels. Amelia inspected the water pump, radiator, hoses, wings' wire bracing, and landing gear. She oiled the valve stems, hoping the ritual of cleaning metal parts would take her mind off the rescue team's spotting a parachute, fluttering, billowing, filling with wind too late, tangling around Marvel Crosson's broken body.

The mechanics arrived by four to double- and triple-check

the planes. All the pilots were ready when light broke through the eastern sky.

Amelia was conscious of the thinnest line between good luck and bad. She flew up cautiously and cruised at a moderate speed. But after fifty miles, she opened the throttle. She pushed the engine a little harder than she should have, but she landed safely that afternoon and again that evening.

In Fort Worth, Texas, Amelia pressed the outstretched hands of strangers as gratefully as if their good wishes had kept her safe. The simple pleasure of being alive made her savor the roast chicken and soft rolls the pilots were served.

Not all of them had been lucky that day. Margaret Perry had checked into a hospital, where she was diagnosed with typhoid fever. Earlier in the day, another pilot flew off course and ran out of fuel, but landed safely. Another lost her maps when they blew out of her open cockpit, but she was able to find her way to the airfield. Worst of all, someone had tossed away a burning cigarette, which fell into the plane belonging to Blanche Noyes. A fire started when she was flying over the desert. She made an emergency landing and put out the flames by scooping up sand, which she tossed onto the fire. Although the plane's wheels had been crushed when she landed so suddenly, and her hands were badly burned, she managed to take off again and fly to the airfield.

Blanche held up her bandaged hands and said, "I lost my chance of winning, but I've been heading for the air show in Cleveland, and I won't stop until I get there."

On the fifth day of the race, Pancho's plane was wrecked

when a strong wind blew it into a truck. Reluctantly, she accepted a ride to Cleveland.

The others pressed on. By the time they reached Indiana, Amelia, Ruth, and Louise were close contenders for first place. Louise had been the first to arrive in Wichita, Kansas, which thrilled her parents and husband, who were there to greet her. Gladys O'Donnell, who'd won some circuit races in the past few years, wasn't far behind.

The next night the pilots stopped in St. Louis. They flew on over Illinois and Indiana to Columbus, where, on the last day of the race, they prepared to fly across Ohio. Amelia pushed her reddish-brown hair off her forehead, though the wind immediately blew it back. She pressed the hands of other pilots, wishing them good luck. She avoided only Ruth.

The planes lined up, with the pilots ready to take off one minute apart, just as they had each morning. A starter waved the red-and-white signal flag. Louise's plane roared over the field and into the sky. Blanche took off smoothly, despite her bandaged hands.

Next, Ruth's silver plane sped down the runway. It wobbled as the wind lifted, then tipped it. It blew across the runway, rolled over, and smashed into a tractor. The broken plane lay with one wing pointing at the sky. The other wing was crushed.

Mechanics rushed to the wrecked plane, while an official raised and lowered the flag to signal Amelia, who was next in line, to go ahead. She gripped the stick and kept her foot on the brakes as she stared at the split wood of Ruth's plane, the torn canvas. The plane's roof was on the runway, with the wheels facing the sky. Ruth must be hanging upside down, held by her seat belt. Would the plane burst into flames?

Amelia jumped out of the cockpit. She ran toward the crushed plane, yelling, "Get out! Ruth, get out of there!"

Ruth crawled slowly out of the wreck. She stood up, but she looked dazed as she stared at the man who still waved a red-and-white flag. Amelia had missed her turn, but one by one, other pilots were flying into the sky.

"Are you all right?" Amelia asked.

"You missed your turn!" Ruth said.

"You are all right." For a moment, tears of relief, or perhaps those she'd held back when Marvel died, clouded Amelia's eyes.

"Don't you want to win?" Ruth asked.

Of course she did, but Amelia had always imagined flying over the finish line with Ruth close behind her. "I need my competitors," she said.

Ruth raised her arms. "Go!" she shouted. "Hurry!"

Amelia ran back to her plane. Within twenty minutes, she'd sped past several planes. The morning stretched before her, filled with opportunity.

Ruth's words echoed in her mind: *Go! Hurry!*

The last lap of the course was short. Soon Lake Erie sparkled as Amelia headed down to the Cleveland airfield, where thousands of women, men, and children waved papers and kerchiefs. The arrival of the women pilots was a bigger

draw than the speed races and exhibitions that were performed throughout the day. Amelia asked who came in first,
then signed autographs and talked to reporters while George
Putnam elbowed his way through the crowd.

"I was checking your time. What happened?" he asked.

Amelia nodded and smiled, while continuing to sign her
name to papers thrust into her hand.

"Louise didn't even get a chance to climb out of her plane
when she landed," George said. "Some men carried her in her
plane onto the middle of the field. The bleachers were packed
with cheering people. That should have been you."

"Louise is shy. I hope she didn't hate that," Amelia said.

"She stood in the cockpit and waved, with a grin all over
her face," George said. His smile was tight, but his white
teeth contrasted pleasantly with his dark hair and tanned
skin. He led Amelia to a quieter part of the packed airfield,
behind refreshment stands and ticket counters. "You came in
third. At least Louise has broken speed and distance records,
but who's ever heard of Gladys O'Donnell?"

"Gladys has won a lot of closed-circuit races, like the ones
they're doing now." Amelia looked overhead, where pilots
flew around pylons held by tall poles. "It's tough racing close
like that. Planes' wings or tails are often clipped by the competitors'. I hope Gladys's husband and kids were here to see
her come in."

"What am I going to tell all the people who thought Lady
Lindy would come in first?"

"Tell them to watch this race next year."

"People won't wait a year."

"It's strange. I thought I'd care more that I didn't come in first. But I enjoyed the race. I made some friends."

"You'll care if your picture stops showing up in papers and you don't get any more speaking jobs. I've been talking with some men from Firebrand Tires about endorsements that could mean thousands of dollars for you. And a fellow who designs hats. We can't tell them you took third place!"

"We'll have to." Amelia linked her arm through his and headed toward the tent set up for the racers.

She saw Louise outside the entrance and gave her a congratulatory hug. "George said you were carried in your plane out onto the field."

"I was more scared when the strangers held up my plane than I was in the sky." Louise grinned.

Ruth stepped out of the tent, wearing a cloche hat pulled down to just above her violet-black eyes. The fringe on the hem of her dress rippled against her legs, which gleamed in silk stockings.

"You look nice." Amelia smiled.

"You mean better than with a plane wrapped around me?" Ruth said. "Congratulations. I heard you placed third."

"You were ahead until today," Amelia said.

Ruth just shrugged, the way racers learn to do, and Amelia quickly added, "I'd like you to meet George Putnam."

George put out his hand, but Ruth said, "We've met."

Amelia looked with surprise at George, who lifted a shoulder.

"You didn't know I was interviewed to become the first woman to cross the Atlantic?" Ruth asked Amelia. Then she looked at George. "Once you found a girl with Lucky Lind-bergh's charm, you never gave me another thought."

They were interrupted by reporters, who were gathering the pilots for a group photo. One said, "Let's get the top three aerial queens now."

Amelia, Gladys, and Louise draped their arms around each other.

"Amelia, give us a smile! Hold up that big trophy."

"That trophy belongs to Louise!" Amelia protested, but it was thrust into her hands. She blinked as the camera flashed.

"Now we want some pictures of just you, Amelia."

"But Louise won first place!" she said.

"The people want Lady Lindy," the reporters said. They snapped more pictures, then left to take pictures of the pilots who were racing in loops above the airfield.

George left, too, and the women ducked back into the tent, where the noise of the fairground was muffled. "It will be strange not to get up at four o'clock tomorrow," Gladys said.

"Back to the gas station." Bobbi frowned. "I'll miss every-thing except the chicken dinners."

"I came in late, but I never had as much fun in my life," Opal added.

"Proportionally, more women who entered this race fin-ished than men who entered and completed their cross-country race," Louise said. "Now men will have to think twice before saying there's something we can't do."

"There's already talk that they'll let us compete with them next year," Gladys said. "But I'd miss this race."

"Except that the prize money for the men's race is ten times as much," Ruth noted.

"I'll miss everyone." Louise's eyes briefly turned sad.

"It doesn't all have to be over," Amelia said. "We need an organization to demand equal pay and opportunities. Men can claim that one extraordinary woman is an exception to be ignored, but they can't pretend they don't see a group of us." She looked at the women who'd changed their lives by flying.

They began making plans. Then their talk was interrupted by the crash of splintering metal, followed by screams and ambulance sirens. The women rushed from the tent and heard that one of the circuit-racing planes had clipped the other's tail, and both planes had gone down.

Most of the women left to find out more, but Amelia and Ruth stayed by the tent. Amelia noticed that Ruth's strong hands were shaking.

"I was all right when my plane cracked up. Now look at me." Ruth shivered, and her eyes turned shiny as she looked up. "I was afraid of heights as a kid. I wouldn't go up elevators or into tall buildings or on roller coasters. Then my dad offered me a plane ride as a present for graduating from high school, and I was too embarrassed to refuse. I went up with an old war pilot. He looped the loop, and I started laughing. It's only air, I thought. Suddenly, I wasn't afraid of heights. I wasn't afraid of anything."

Amelia noticed that Ruth's hands were quiet again as she said, "I didn't win anything, but I still want a hot fudge sundae. Want to join me?"

"Sure." Amelia walked beside her, then said, "Ruth, I'm sorry."

"What for?"

"The crash. And my trip across the Atlantic. You should have gone. You had more flying experience than I did."

"A lot more," Ruth agreed. "But the ocean's still there. I'll fly across it first."

"What makes you think I'm planning to fly to Europe?"

"You're a pilot. Riding as a passenger could never be enough." Ruth looked her friend and rival in the eye. "They say Paris is lovely in the springtime."

"I'll let you know." Amelia smiled.

—

That fall of 1929, women pilots from around the country met at the Curtiss Airfield on Long Island. Sitting in the storage loft of the hangar, they sipped tea and ate cookies served from a toolbox wagon, and founded an organization of women pilots that would help open more aviation jobs to women. They planned bake sales and airplane washes to raise scholarships so more women could learn to fly. And they discussed making memorials so that pilots like Marvel Crosson wouldn't be forgotten.

They argued about a name. Amelia winced at some suggestions: Birdwomen, Lady Birds, and Lady Buzzards. She shook her head at Sky Girls, the Angels Club, Climbing Vines, and Sky Scrapers. Finally she suggested that they keep it simple. They'd send information around the country, see how many women joined, and use the total number of charter members for their name.

The year after the Ninety-Nines was founded, barely a day went by when Amelia and Ruth didn't think about crossing the Atlantic. In 1930, Amelia set a women's speed record, which Ruth broke a few months later. Amelia spent most of the next year in airfields, staying on the ground just long enough to marry George Putnam, who'd agreed that she should keep her name and independence.

That year, Ruth broke her back when her plane crashed. Doctors fitted her into a steel cast that went from her armpits to the top of her thighs. Ruth was in constant pain, but she had straps hung from the top of her cockpit. When the pain in her lower back grew too intense, she eased the pressure by hoisting herself from the straps.

Before she was out of her cast, Ruth had set a date to cross the ocean. Then one day, in midair, a leaking valve set her plane's fuel tank on fire. She managed to land the plane and scramble out of the cockpit seconds before the tank exploded.

While Ruth's plane was being fixed, Amelia set off for Europe in her red Lockheed Vega. After about the first six hours, her eyes grew sore as she gazed at moonlight and clouds, but she couldn't shut them for a second. Then rain fell. Lightning flashed over the sea, wind rocked the plane, and Amelia's sleepiness vanished. Her plane sank as the wings became coated with heavy ice. She dipped down for the warmer temperatures just above the waves, hoping one wouldn't suddenly rise. The water could soak the wooden body and wings of the plane and make it too heavy to fly.

Her altimeter broke, so she couldn't tell exactly how far she was above the ocean. She guided the plane back up again, until slush darkened the windshield and she had to fly closer to the waves for a while. Then the tachometer broke, so she wasn't sure how fast she was going, and that made it hard to estimate how far she had to go. The exhaust manifold, which channels smoke from burning fuel out of the plane, cracked. When a tank leaked and gas dripped onto Amelia's left shoulder, the exposed flames grew dangerous. If the fuel caught fire, the plane could explode. Amelia decided to fly closer to the ocean, since she preferred drowning to burning.

Finally Amelia saw a small fishing boat and knew the shore couldn't be far away. She landed in a cow pasture in Northern Ireland, where she told a farmer, "I've come from America."

"Have ye now?" he said, then borrowed a car to drive her to a neighbor with a phone.

In London, she was celebrated as the first woman to pilot a plane across the Atlantic, the second person since Charles Lindbergh to make the trip flying solo. She took a ship back to New York, where planes swooped above the harbor to bombard her with bouquets. Parades with bands and screeching whistles and blaring horns took over New York City streets. People tossed ticker tape and pages ripped from phone books.

Amelia grinned, exposing the gap between her front teeth, though already she was thinking of other challenges.

Photographers snapped pictures, which girls and women studied while shaping dreams of their own.

PART III
FRIENDSHIPS AND WAR
(1932-44)

 young woman with carefully bleached and styled hair strode up to a desk in the hangar at Roosevelt Air Field on Long Island. An instructor introduced himself as Husky, took out a form, and asked her name.

"Jacqueline Cochran."

"Nice name."

She smiled. She'd thought so, too, when she picked it from a phone book.

"Should I write 'Miss' or 'Mrs.'?" Husky asked.

"What difference does it make? I'm applying for flying lessons, not a date."

"We need to know how you plan to pay for lessons. How old are you?"

"I'm twenty-one," she said. Or close enough. Her foster parents had never been sure of her exact birthday. "Can we get into a plane now?"

"Don't be in such a hurry." Husky shook his head. "Every time Amelia Earhart gets her picture in the papers, girls come in here thinking all they have to do is cut their hair and tie a scarf around their necks and they're pilots."

Reading about Amelia Earhart's flight had inspired Jackie, but she wasn't looking for thrills. While she liked her job at a Saks Fifth Avenue salon, she didn't plan to cut and curl hair forever. She saw more money in selling beauty products, and if she was going to travel around the country doing that, she couldn't waste time in cars or trains.

Jackie hadn't yet begun her business, but it was important to make plans. She'd grown up in a one-room shack, where she slept on the dirt floor and wore dresses made from flour sacks. She'd taught herself to read by sounding out the names painted on the trains that passed on the tracks behind the family cabin. Jackie had hoped to please her foster parents, who worked in the Florida sawmills, by tidying up the cabin, but her efforts only made them say, "What makes you think you're better than us?" She suspected she'd been taken in mostly to mind the babies of her teenaged foster sisters while they worked at the mill.

Jackie left school by fifth grade and took jobs cleaning houses, until a woman she worked for asked her to mix hair dyes and curling solutions at her beauty parlor. Within a few years, Jackie had learned enough about the business to work her way up to one of the fanciest salons in New York.

"I know what I'm doing," Jackie told Husky. "I've been reading a book about how to fly."

He rolled his eyes.

"Are you going to give me lessons, or should I find another teacher?" Jackie asked.

Husky shrugged and led her to a trainer plane with two sets of controls. He sounded bored as he explained the function of the instruments. He showed Jackie how to push on the brakes and pull back the stick while he swung the propellers. Then he hopped in. Jackie wondered if the small plane could rise under their weight. They bumped along the runway, but the ride turned smooth once the sky was all around them.

As they circled the field, Jackie watched her teacher's hands. Perhaps his movements simply matched the instructions she was studying, but they seemed to be something she'd always known.

"Can we go faster?" she shouted, but her voice was drowned out by the engine's roar. She spun her hands to signal speed.

Husky opened the throttle, and Jackie laughed as they zipped above the airfield. Clouds were more beautiful close up. Trees and fields looked lovelier from a distance.

"I want to try." She pointed to her set of controls.

Husky shrugged.

Jackie set her small feet on the rudder. As she grasped the stick with one hand and the throttle with the other, power ran from her hands through her body. She flew over the field, then brought down the plane with few bumps.

They got out, and Jackie smoothed her blond hair back in place. "I'm going to pay for a full set of lessons," she said. "I've saved up three weeks of vacation time. I want my license by the time I go back to work."

"Are you crazy?" Husky asked. "It takes even the best students three or four months of practice before they're ready to handle a plane alone."

"I learned to drive a car in a day."

"Airplanes are complicated. In the sky, one mistake can be your last."

"I'm a working girl. I don't have a few months to fool around. And I just met a fellow who bet me the cost of lessons that I couldn't earn a license so quickly. Now, come on. We're wasting time."

Jackie spent the afternoon using the stick to lift or lower the nose of the plane. She pushed the rudder bar with her feet to turn the plane. The concentration was hard, but blissful.

As Jackie headed back to her apartment after dark, she thought that no one had ever bought a dress especially for her. No one had ever set the table for her or asked what she'd like for lunch. No one knew her birthday or had ever lit a candle and said, "Make a wish." But now the sky had opened before her, the home she'd never had.

The next morning, Jackie took the first train to the airport and arrived just after dawn. It was already hot. The place was deserted, so Jackie looked at the sky, which, like herself, seemed changed since yesterday: bigger and more full of possibility. She wandered into the hangar, past locked offices and a snack bar.

Behind a row of airplanes, a young woman stood on scaffolding, examining a huge canvas that was stretched across a wall. About half the mural was filled with sketches or paintings of early airplanes and aviators.

The limber, dark-haired artist swung down from the platform and picked up a jar of water. She held out her hand and said, "I'm Aline Rhonie."

"Jacqueline Cochran. Everyone calls me Jackie." She looked at the canvas and said, "I didn't know a painting could be so big."

"It's too easy for people to miss a small painting. And I want to include twenty years of history by the time I'm done." Aline wiped a kerchief across her sweaty forehead, then pointed toward the far left of the canvas. "You probably recognize the Wright brothers. There's Blanche Scott, the first woman to fly, and Harriet Quimby in her purple-hooded outfit."

"You must get here early so you can stop working before the noon heat," Jackie said.

"It is cooler in the morning, but I'll work all day." Aline's voice was cheerful. "I've got hundreds more people and planes to include, and I can't stop because of weather. It's harder in winter because the hangar isn't heated. My hands get stiff with the cold, though I wear my fleece-lined flying suit."

"You're a pilot, too?"

"When I was learning to fly, I liked thinking about the

pilots who came before me." Aline nodded, climbed up the scaffolding, picked up her paintbrush, and said, "Nice to meet you."

Jackie examined planes until Husky arrived, and they climbed into the light trainer. In the sky, Husky took the plane through rapid loops, spins, and rolls. Jackie guessed that he was trying to scare her, but she held on and enjoyed the ride. When they landed, Husky peered at her face as if he hoped her skin had turned green.

"Want to go get a hot dog and soda?" she asked.

After their snack, Jackie learned how to accelerate while climbing into the sky and how to shut off the power when coming down. She practiced slips, stalls, and spins to prepare for a forced landing.

They stopped when it began to get dark. Jackie said, "I'm ready to fly by myself tomorrow."

"Nobody goes solo after two days!" Husky protested.

But the next afternoon, at three o'clock, Jackie took up the plane by herself. Away from others' voices and glances, she felt a power she'd never known surge through her hands. With one motion she could save or lose her life. She was alone, yet she had never felt less lonely.

She still had a lot to learn, but she already knew that nothing could keep her from the sky. Not even fear, which she felt two days later while watching mechanics remove a wrecked plane from the airstrip. An ambulance came for the body.

That could happen to me, Jackie thought, and then she pushed the thought away. *He must have been careless. His plane was different*. The possibility of death was always close. A pilot had to know that a second of hesitation, the briefest lapse of nerve, could end her life. Jackie learned to open the throttle with a quick, silent prayer and to keep her eyes straight ahead.

Two weeks later, Jackie called the friend who'd bet her that she couldn't earn a pilot's license in three weeks. "Is there anywhere you need to go?" Jackie asked. "Can I offer you a ride?"

"This is the first bet I ever made that I'm happy to lose," Floyd Odlum replied. "And yes, there are plenty of places I'd like to see."

As the months passed, Jackie and Floyd spent more and more time together. Floyd told Jackie that he'd grown up as one of five children of a minister, borrowed money for college, then become very successful in law and business. He lent her money to help her start Jacqueline Cochran Cosmetics.

It wasn't easy to set up a company while training to be a top pilot, but the fears Jackie conquered in the air made her a more confident saleswoman, and her business successes made her fly with more bravado. She flew from city to city, selling face creams and lipsticks. Sitting in a cockpit for long hours seemed no reason for a lady not to look her best, but there was barely room for a comb in the pocket of a flight suit. So Jackie designed a small tube that held powder, rouge, eye shadow, and perfume. Because high altitudes and strong winds dried skin and chapped lips, she developed moisturizers and lip balms. "Wings to Beauty" became her company's slogan.

Floyd told Jackie that life with her would never be boring. Jackie agreed that their lives could be filled with adventure, but when Floyd proposed, she said, "People will say I'm marrying you for your money."

"When did you start caring about what people think?"

"You grew up poor, but at least you knew your parents. We're talking about having children, and I don't even know where I came from."

"I know you've always felt uneasy about your past." Floyd took a sealed envelope from his pocket. "I took the liberty of hiring someone to find out a few things about your real mother. All the facts he found are here. It's up to you whether or not to open it. You can burn it, for all I care. Jackie, I may not know your mother or father, but I believe that if they met you, they'd be very, very proud."

Jackie tucked away the envelope, unopened. A few months later, she and Floyd were married. Jackie kept the name she'd chosen, so when they combined the property she'd bought in California with Floyd's larger piece of land and built a home, they called it the Cochran-Odlum Ranch. They bought an apartment in New York City, too, and had the entryway floor made to look like a compass. Their life together would be on the move. Jackie aimed to travel in all directions.

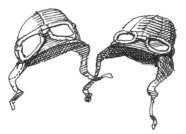

F lying fast made Jackie Cochran want to fly faster. Not long after she'd learned to fly, Jackie started racing planes. Soon after she began racing, she began to come in first. Once she had a shelfful of trophies, she wanted a whole case of them; once she had a caseful, she began filling a room devoted to her ribbons and awards.

Jackie knew that some women pilots had spent years urging Vincent Bendix and other race sponsors to let them be included in the annual men's cross-country air race. She tried a different tactic. She got a list of the enrolled racers, then telephoned each one, asking if he'd mind if she entered. When she informed Vincent Bendix that not a single pilot objected to her competing, he agreed that she could race. Amelia Earhart signed on, too.

The race began on September 2, 1935, in Los Angeles, California. Instead of resting for the race, which would begin after midnight, Jackie spent the afternoon shopping for a dress to wear at the end, in Cleveland, Ohio. She returned to the airfield to find out that the new engine in her plane was overheating. Both the manager of the race and the head of the company that had made the engine urged Jackie to cancel. But Jackie worried that if she didn't fly, people might think not only that she'd lost her nerve but that women couldn't fly under tough conditions.

Jackie was looking over the dark and foggy airfield when Amelia Earhart and her husband, George Putnam, walked over.

"Jackie, I've been wanting to meet you!" Amelia said. "Thank you for helping us get into this race."

After spending years chatting in beauty parlors, Jackie had learned how to make conversation, but she felt a bit tongue-tied in front of this famous flier. She thought Amelia had a grace and energy that her photographs didn't catch, but she focused on her unbrushed hair and her skin, which was tanned and roughened from sun and wind. Amelia's long fingers were elegant, but she could use a good manicure. Jackie had the urge to check her own makeup and hair to make sure that the too-thin girl wearing dresses made from flour sacks wasn't showing.

"So you're the girl with the 13 painted on her airplane," George Putnam said.

"The number 13 brings me luck." Jackie's voice was

chilly. She'd heard how George convinced his publisher friends to print news about Amelia on the front pages and made sure that accomplishments of other women aviators were pushed to the back, if they appeared at all.

"I guess we'll all need luck," Amelia said. "The fog's so thick that you can't see from one side of the airport to the other."

Jackie excused herself to check her plane. Once again, the owner of the company that had made her engine warned her there could be a problem, but since he wasn't willing to tell reporters that, Jackie decided to stay in the race. Waiting her turn, Jackie watched Amelia and other pilots take off. Around three o'clock in the morning, one pilot sped down the runway. Jackie heard a crash, and flames pierced the fog. Fire trucks arrived too late to pull out the pilot alive.

While the wrecked plane was hauled from the runway, Jackie fastened her seat belt and faced the panel of nearly one hundred levers. She had memorized the control board so she could reach for the right lever even in the dark. She didn't want to waste the half second it would take to flick on a light switch while she took off.

Jackie taxied down the runway. An ambulance and fire truck hurried behind her, to be close by if she crashed. As she rose into the air, her plane felt strangely heavy. It vibrated as she set out through the fog, but she managed to get it high enough to cross the Rocky Mountains. Then, instead of going faster over the desert, she had to keep decreasing her speed. Even so, the plane shook harder and harder. Jackie wondered how and where she would land if the motor failed.

Shortly after flying over the Grand Canyon, which looked deep and forbidding, she turned her plane around.

Jackie didn't win or even finish the race, but she showed that she wasn't afraid to fly under bad conditions. And she lived to wear her new dress, if not in Cleveland. Amelia placed fifth, a good enough showing to make it likely that women would compete again in next year's cross-country race.

Jackie returned to work in New York, where, a few weeks later, she got a call from Amelia.

"I heard you had engine trouble," Amelia said. "I'm sorry."

"It was nothing much, but I decided not to take a chance."

"You're a true pilot. You never blame your plane."

"A real pilot knows not only how to fly but when to head back to the ground. I want to have grandchildren someday to tell my stories to."

"Mmm. Did you hear I got a new plane, a Lockheed Electra with all the latest gauges and equipment? It's from Purdue University, where I've been giving some lectures. They call it a flying laboratory."

"I'd love to see that!"

"Jackie, I need to get in some long-distance practice with it. Why don't you fly out to California with me? It would be safer and faster with a copilot."

"You'd let me take the controls of your new plane? You hardly know me."

"I've heard a lot about you. I can't think of anyone I'd trust more."

"But can I trust you?"

Amelia laughed. "So I had a few crack-ups when I was younger. I'm more cautious now."

A few weeks afterward, Jackie packed several suitcases, which she took to the airport. Accustomed to keeping the weight on her plane low to set long-distance records, Amelia had one small bag. She showed Jackie the features of the two-engine plane, which had been designed to hold six passengers, though its seats had been taken out to make room for more gas tanks.

Jackie climbed in beside Amelia. She watched Amelia's hands on the controls and instinctively memorized the placement and function of levers and gauges. The noise of the two engines made it impossible to talk, but Jackie looked out the windows as they crossed the earth at about two hundred miles per hour. The sky's colors and clouds changed moment by moment. Rivers, roads, and hills below made a beautiful map.

They stopped at an airport for lunch, then Jackie took the controls. Her heart beat faster, and her blood seemed to flow more quickly than it did on the ground, as if her body were racing to keep up with the plane. The hum and rumble of the engines told her how hard to press the levers. She headed west, where dark clouds were massing together. Rain began to fall, which made it hard to see ahead. Jackie waved toward the ground to signal Amelia that she thought they should land early. Amelia shook her head. But as rain streamed over the windshield, Jackie looked for the nearest airport. Amelia shrugged, and Jackie headed down.

They found a rooming house where they could spend the night. The next morning was overcast; then it rained as they

traveled to St. Louis. They found an inn for the night, and when they woke in the morning, it was obvious that the stormy skies would be dangerous to navigate.

Jackie settled in her room to write business letters and work out schedules to accommodate both air races and staff meetings for her cosmetics company. When lightning struck some power lines and knocked out the electricity, the innkeepers lit old gas lamps. Jackie worked in her room until she heard a knock.

Amelia held up her travel bag. "The innkeeper said the storm has stranded a lot of folks in the city, and they're pressed for room. Do you mind if we share? I've slept on floors before. You can't be a pilot and care too much about comfort."

"All right, but I have letters to write." When Jackie had accepted Amelia's offer to fly in her plane, she'd known the cockpit would be too noisy for talk. She couldn't help admiring Amelia, but she didn't have much time in her life for a friend.

Amelia unpacked, tossing out a miniature American flag and a slender leather bracelet embedded with silver clouds. "No matter how small my bag is, there's always room for my good-luck charms." She smiled. "I hoped you'd show up at one of our Ninety-Nine meetings. We could use more women like you."

"I'm too busy for clubs. My business demands long hours. It's more than putting my name on the products," Jackie said as a jab at Amelia, who licensed her name to sell hats, spark plugs, and motor oil. "Besides, I don't see the point of women organizing separately from men. I want to be the best—of either sex."

"So do I," Amelia said. "Not just in the United States, but

in the world. But until women are allowed to train in the military and get jobs that are closed to us now, we're handicapped. Everyone gets some help. When Neta Snook, my first flight teacher, knew I was serious, she kept giving me lessons even after I ran out of money. The best way to pay her back is by making sure that the women who come after us don't have to keep proving, over and over, that we can do what men can." Amelia focused her gray eyes on Jackie. "You said you wanted grandchildren. If those girls want to be pilots, wouldn't it be great if they could just get in a plane without anyone making a fuss?"

Jackie looked back at her papers. She was sorry she'd ever said anything about grandchildren to anyone, since Floyd's and her efforts to have children kept failing.

Amelia stepped closer to the window and said, "Maybe we should just risk the weather and go. The rain has got to start slowing down."

"Are you crazy?" Jackie said.

"Don't pilots have to be a little crazy? Besides, I'm tired of waiting."

"So you want to kill me?"

"I'd be in the plane, too." Tiny wrinkles appeared around Amelia's bright eyes. "You think my life has always been easy, don't you?"

"Hasn't it? You're pretty, you're smart. You were a wanted child."

"And what about you, Jackie? You've won dozens of awards. You have a loving husband, a New York penthouse, and a ranch in California."

"I'm not complaining."

"You're just saying that I'm spoiled. I've been lucky, but no one's life is perfect. Sure, I rode horses and raced sleds as a kid, but then my father started coming home from work right after lunch. He needed help to just stumble through the door. When he lost jobs, we pretended he was on vacation."

"He drank?"

Amelia nodded.

Jackie took a deep breath, so her voice was soft as she said, "And now you're the most famous woman in the world."

"Maybe. Jackie, I crossed one ocean, but there are other seas. The Pacific is even bigger."

Jackie smiled, thinking of how she and Amelia had come from different worlds, but were in the same place now. She'd never met anyone whose ambition was as big as hers.

"I had nothing, growing up in a little mill town." Jackie put down her papers and began to tell a story she'd kept secret. "I didn't even know to want much, until a yellow-haired doll showed up in the general store one day. It was being raffled off. You got a ticket for every twenty-five cents you spent. I was about eight years old, but was taking care of my foster sister's little girl, Willie Mae. I took her around to neighbors as I earned a penny here, a nickel there, scrubbing floors and hanging up wash and running errands. By Christmas Eve, I'd earned enough to get two tickets. A crowd gathered to see who was the winner. My name was called." Jackie closed her eyes for a second, remembering how she'd held out her arms, then touched the doll's bristly lashes, attached to eyelids that opened and shut, the small smooth hands and shiny shoes.

Jackie looked at Amelia and continued, "Three-year-old

Willie Mae cried. She begged for the doll. My foster mother said I was too old for toys. My father grabbed my doll and gave it to Willie Mae."

"Jackie, I'm sorry," Amelia said.

"Don't be," Jackie said. "Willie Mae is grown up now. She called me a while back and said she'd seen my name in the papers. She has a little girl of her own now, but her husband didn't stick around. Things are tough."

"What did you say?" Amelia asked.

"I asked if she still had that doll."

Amelia lifted her eyebrows.

"No one gets something for nothing," Jackie said. "I gave Willie Mae a handout. She gave me back the doll."

"You seem to have a knack for getting what you want." Amelia smiled.

"So do you."

"Jackie, I want to be the first person to circle the world at the equator."

"You'd choose the greatest distance around the world?" Jackie asked.

"If I didn't fly at the widest possible point, someone could go at a wider latitude and break my record. No one has done this, Jackie. No man, no woman."

Jackie nodded. They continued to talk, read, and write through the following two days. When the weather cleared, they set out, though more bad weather held them up in Texas. By the time they'd reached California, Jackie knew she had a friend who loved the sky as much as she did. She invited her to visit the ranch sometime.

Within a few months, Amelia told Jackie that she'd found a navigator to accompany her around the world in the Lockheed Electra. Not much later, Amelia called and said, "I suppose you heard I cracked up my plane while taking off from Hawaii. It wasn't properly loaded, and it tipped in the wind. It's going to take a while to get it fixed, so I was wondering if your invitation to visit your ranch is still open. My homes are surrounded by reporters. Besides, I'd like your company."

"I'll fix up a spare bedroom," Jackie said.

Jackie knew that Amelia must be constantly thinking about her upcoming flight, but they didn't discuss it while playing tennis and golf, riding horses, and swimming in the pool. Jackie showed Amelia her room full of trophies and ribbons, her collections of fairy tales, and the golden-haired doll she'd won, lost, and gotten back. Walking past lemon and orange trees, they talked about the troubled times in Europe, where Germany, ruled by Adolf Hitler's Nazi Party, was threatening neighboring countries.

"Ever since I was a nurse to soldiers, I've been against war of any kind," Amelia said.

"Force is the only thing rulers like Hitler understand," Jackie said. "And airplanes make the world seem smaller. What happens in one country affects us all."

"If we do go into war, I'd like to see women fighting, too. Maybe women in combat would make battles less thrilling for men, and wars would finally stop."

For a week, they talked about almost everything except Amelia's upcoming flight. But when Amelia heard that her plane was nearly ready, Jackie bent over the maps that Amelia spread on the carpet beside the fireplace.

Jackie traced the shape of India, and ran a finger across Africa. "Someday I'd like to see the world," she said. "But, Amelia, maybe that crack-up in Hawaii was a sign you shouldn't go. It's not only the length of the trip that's a challenge. You'll be above oceans and jungles and deserts, none of them a good place for your luck to run out. You may run into bad storms in the monsoon season."

"If it was easy, somebody would have done it already."

"I heard that your navigator crashed a car not too long ago. And it wasn't the first time."

"Fred Noonan has stopped drinking." Amelia looked up from the map of the world.

"A drinking problem doesn't just go away," Jackie said. "You know that."

"I didn't realize you listened so much to other people."

"I do when they make sense."

"Eleanor Roosevelt cabled me a warning. Louise Thaden is flying out to try to talk me out of it, too. As if she's one to put safety first! She won her last race by using a gas tank that was so big it blocked the exit to her plane."

"Wait at least a few months, maybe another year. They're making better radios every day. If something happened, you'd want to be able to get a message through the air waves. If you have to make an emergency landing, you'll be in some of the most unpopulated parts of the world."

"I can't wait. If I don't leave in the next week, the trade winds will change. George has scheduled places where I'll stop, and he expects me back in New York for the Fourth of July celebrations. This trip is expensive. I need all the publicity I can get to pay the bills."

"So you'll risk your life to get to a parade?"

"I don't have children to worry about. I've sent money to my mother and sister."

"And your husband?"

"If something happens, George will find another wife within a year." Amelia twisted her narrow leather bracelet with the silver clouds. "I don't want to pick up the newspaper one morning and find out that Ruth Nichols has headed out around the world. Jackie, I thought you of all people would understand that breaking one record only makes you want to take on a bigger challenge."

Jackie looked at the woman who'd come to her ranch to enjoy horses and water and the scent of grass. The days right before a flight were not the time to worry. She stood, opened a drawer, and handed Amelia a bag. "I bought a kite that you can send up as a signal if your plane goes down. There's a knife with all sorts of gadgets and some fishing line and hooks. Just in case."

Amelia nodded her thanks, and untied the scarf she wore around her neck. "I want you to have something of mine, too. I'll sign it, if you want."

"Sign it when you come back," Jackie said.

Amelia wrote her name across the scarf and handed it to Jackie.

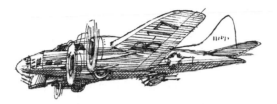

Once again, Amelia flew across the Atlantic Ocean. She flew over the deserts and forests of Africa and through monsoons over Asia. She stopped in Australia, then headed north over the Pacific Ocean. She'd flown about twenty thousand miles and was close to the end of her journey when a call for help came over the radio from Amelia. She couldn't locate the small island where she was supposed to get more fuel.

Alarmed friends telephoned Jackie with the news that President Franklin D. Roosevelt had ordered ships and airplanes to look for the plane, which must have run out of gas and crashed. Jackie took out her map of the Pacific and located the mile-long island where Amelia had planned to land. Amid the big blue space, Howland Island was marked with a dot. Jackie learned that Amelia had left behind her parachute, since any extra weight would use up fuel. She had even left behind her leather bracelet with silver clouds, which weighed almost nothing.

After three days of the biggest sea search ever made, there was no sign of a broken wing or even a scrap of metal. Army and navy men would keep looking, but Jackie went to church and lighted candles. Soon she joined the Ninety-Nines, became its president, and worked with Ruth Nichols to set up an Amelia Earhart Scholarship Fund for women pilots. But Jackie couldn't think of a way to truly honor her friend until, in 1941, the United States joined the Allies in World War II. Jackie put on her classiest suit and a bracelet with a diamond sun, moon, and stars, and met President Roosevelt and his wife, Eleanor, for lunch. She told them about her idea for a women's air force.

"One woman can do a lot, but a group can do even more," Jackie said. "I didn't get where I am by myself."

"This is our war, too," Eleanor Roosevelt agreed. "Women make up half of the country. We can't afford not to use their talents."

President Roosevelt had some doubts, but he promised to send a note supporting Jackie's plan to General H. H. "Hap" Arnold, who was in charge of building the Army Air Force.

Jackie headed straight to the Pentagon.

"I want to win this fight against the Nazis as much as you do, but the public isn't ready to see women in military planes," General Arnold said.

"We wouldn't have to fly in combat, but we could pilot

planes to factories and air bases, leaving men more time to prepare for battles," Jackie said.

"How can I put you in charge of a group of military fliers? Jackie, you never even graduated from high school."

"If I could teach myself to fly when I could barely read, I can teach other women," Jackie said. "I came from nowhere and started up my own successful business."

"Running a cosmetics company isn't the same as leading an army."

"I know how to give orders and delegate responsibility. I know flying."

"I can't argue with that. I've heard you've broken more speed and altitude records than any other man or woman." General Arnold smiled. "You're stubborn."

"I didn't get where I am by being nice."

"Good. Heading a military unit doesn't make one popular."

"You mean . . . ?"

"Nothing," General Arnold said. "All I can promise is that I'll keep you in mind if something comes up."

Not long afterward, he asked her to fly a bomber plane across the Atlantic. Jackie stayed in England, where the British had been at war long enough for many people to have been killed, and they accepted any help they could get. Jackie joined British women ferrying planes from factories to air bases.

In 1942, General Arnold called Jackie back to the United States to start a program like the one in England. Jackie asked some of her cosmetics company staff to look through files for the names of every woman who'd been a member of the Ninety-Nines or had earned a pilot's license. She sent out advertisements for women to train as military pilots. Applicants were warned that they wouldn't be paid much. The work would be risky. Some of them would die.

Bags and bags of mail were hauled into Jackie's office.

Twenty-five thousand women wanted to fly.

Jackie flew around the country to interview women between the ages of eighteen and twenty-eight. Some had spent hundreds of hours in the air, while others had only the minimum required experience. They had to be strong enough to pilot for long hours, often with little sleep. Candidates had to be at least five foot two, so that their legs could reach the planes' pedals, but Jackie knew that some doctors doing physicals glanced away while the women stood on tiptoes. One woman hung upside down before her exam, and, in order to add a necessary inch, asked a friend to drive her to the doctor's office while she stretched flat across the backseat.

The women who were selected paid their own way to Texas for training. Some had just graduated from high school, while others had college degrees. Most of the first class were single women, but some were wives, many with husbands overseas. Others were widows of soldiers killed in the war. A few were mothers, who left their children with grandmothers or aunts. The women had quit work as teachers, singers, air traffic controllers, stunt pilots, scientists, and nurses. Each of them worried if she would make it through the rigorous training. Each wondered where she would be sent to fly. But every woman was proud to think that she'd be climbing into a plane, rather than standing in a depot or air-field waving goodbye to someone else.

Jackie hired Dedie Deaton to be in charge of lodging, schedules, and any personal needs of the young women. Mrs. Deaton assigned each trainee a cot and a small foot locker in the barracks. She showed the women where the iron was kept, doled out aspirin, and confiscated radios when the energetic women danced the jitterbug late at night. Even after dark, the Texas heat was often over a hundred degrees in the summer, so Mrs. Deaton let the trainees move their cots outside to catch a breeze. But when tarantulas, scorpions, and black widow spiders were spotted, the women decided to put up with the heat indoors.

The women were called WASPs, for Women's Airforce Service Pilots. They weren't officially part of the military, but they followed army rules and trained like army men. No uni-forms had been issued to the women yet, so they wore men's coveralls, which they belted tightly to hold up the extra fab-ric. They tucked the long cuffs into cowboy boots and rolled up the sleeves. They did jumping jacks, push-ups, and chin-ups after an early breakfast, then marched around the base, breathing in the scents of sagebrush, gasoline, and oil. Dur-ing the afternoons, they took classes in navigation, Morse code, and engine design and repair. They learned how to check the planes' tires for air pressure, the tanks for leaks, and the brakes for signs of wear. Before taking tests, some women tossed coins into a stone fountain they called the wishing well.

Finally they flew up with an instructor. The sky over the

air base was often filled with as many as fifty planes, which made navigating a challenge. The women practiced on more than a dozen different types of aircraft, from one-engine planes to heavy bombers. A few women couldn't tolerate the military discipline or master the planes and went home. But the "washout" rate was in the same proportion to men who left army training camps.

Most of the women couldn't wait to fly alone. When one landed after her first solo flight, a classmate rang the old fire bell. Others dropped what they were doing and raced over to congratulate the pilot. Laughing and shouting, they lifted her over their heads, carried her to the wishing well, and tossed her in. She stood knee-deep in water, dripping wet, grinning, and feeling very, very proud.

Jackie was often away from the air base, as she made plans from her office in the Pentagon or flew around the country to interview candidates for future classes. But she returned when the first class lined up for graduation. Jackie pinned silver wings onto the graduates' white blouses. She spoke to them and to the audience, which included mothers who had put aside a bit of grocery money every week to pay for their daughters' flying lessons. One mother used to drive her daughter to the airport, since she was too young to earn a driver's license, then wait in the car, knitting an afghan, while her daughter swooped and soared overhead.

New classes had already started when the first WASPs began to ferry planes around the country. Most Americans admired their patriotic spirit, and when one pilot was told to leave a restaurant because women wearing trousers weren't allowed, every soldier there pushed back his chair and followed.

But as Amelia Earhart had predicted, some military men resented seeing women enter places where once only men had been allowed. They wrote special rules for them, such as an order that no menstruating woman should pilot a plane. The WASPs were outraged when they were told to report the dates of their periods to the authorities. But when one mentioned that some women could go months or even years without a cycle, everyone nodded, and months passed without a single WASP reporting a period. No flights were delayed or canceled.

Jackie got permission to order uniforms from one of the best designers in New York. Rather than use surplus cloth from the Army, she insisted on fabric the deep blue of a twilight sky for a beret, a fitted jacket, and a straight skirt.

Not long after these arrived, Jackie was asked to select twenty-five of the best pilots for further training and duties at Camp Davis in North Carolina. There, some WASPs instructed new Army Air Force pilots. Others attached long cloth targets to the backs of their planes and zigzagged through the sky while soldiers in training practiced shooting with live ammunition. Some of these bullets missed the targets and pierced the metal of the planes.

The women accepted the dangers of their jobs towing targets, but as the weeks passed, Jackie heard more and more reports about the unsafe condition of the planes they piloted. Engines quit in midair, and the women had to struggle to steer their planes down to the crowded airfield. Some planes had flaps that wouldn't budge. The pilots flew in designated sections of the sky so that they wouldn't hit one another, and when their radios broke, they couldn't be warned if someone flew in their way. One bomber had a canopy—the movable roof of the cockpit—that stuck, so after landing, the pilot had to wait for a passerby to unlatch it.

Jackie was disturbed by the reports, but she knew that all mechanics were overworked during wartime. No planes were in tiptop condition. The sticking canopy seemed merely a nuisance until one woman died because of it. When another pilot cracked her skull when her plane crashed, Jackie flew to North Carolina. She'd heard that the worst planes and the most incompetent teachers were assigned to the women. Some women claimed that they were snubbed or ridiculed. One soldier hated women pilots so much that he put sugar in a gas tank so the plane would crash.

The military leaders at Camp Davis spoke first. They denied that any plane had been sabotaged. They stated that their safety records were impeccable, and that the women were treated fairly.

"Tell me about the pilot who died," Jackie asked the women.

"I was flying over the beach when I saw a plane stall in midair," said Marion Hanrahan. "It hovered for less than a second before it crashed and burst into flames."

Mabel Rawlinson, a librarian from Michigan, had been flying the plane with the canopy that stuck. She must have banged against the roof that wouldn't budge as smoke filled her lungs and flames burned through her clothing and skin.

"We heard her scream," said a woman who'd watched.

Jackie kept her face calm, unreadable, as she thought of how these women worked together, ate together, and slept in cots beside one another. It must have been awful to hear the muffled cries of a woman they'd seen spread jam on her toast hours before. It must have been difficult to pack the shoes she'd left touching and pointing away from the bed, military style, and the novel with a scrap of paper marking the place where she'd stopped reading.

"There's a war on," Jackie said. "All planes have problems."

"We need more mechanics here to fix the planes," Marion Hanrahan said.

"I'll see what I can do, but the whole country is short of workers," Jackie replied.

"That's all you can do?" Marion demanded. "That's all you can say?"

"I hope things will improve, but I can't make any promises," Jackie said.

"That's not good enough." Marion stood up. "I quit."

Jackie stared at the woman with wide, courageous eyes and slightly trembling hands. She admired Marion for demanding the safety standards she deserved. But if this young woman left, congressmen and reporters might ask why a top pilot had quit the program. News of the death and calamities could shut down the WASP program.

"I will not accept your resignation," Jackie told her. Her heart beat hard as Marion sat down and the discussion continued a while longer.

The next day, Jackie flew back to Washington, D.C., where she asked for safer planes. She told General Hap Arnold, "You've got to at least make the WASP an official part of the Armed Forces. Mabel Rawlinson died while serving her country, but we don't have government money to send her body home to Michigan. There's a woman in the hospital with head injuries, and no military insurance to pay the doctors."

"We've sent bills to Congress asking to make the WASP an official part of the Army," General Arnold said. "I'm sorry, Jackie, but things move slowly in Washington."

Once again, Jackie had to wait, though more women died and there were no military trumpets, no flyovers, not even an American flag to drape the coffin or put in the hands of grieving parents. The women's friends held funerals before the sun rose, which was the only free time they had in their full schedules. If the family of the woman who died didn't have much money, the WASPs passed a hat to collect cash to buy a plain pine coffin and send the body home.

The WASPs continued to ferry planes, flying every sort of plane the Air Force owned. Some flew B-29s, the largest bombers built. Others flew the B-26, which was nicknamed the "flying coffin." They simulated bombing attack flights, delivered cargo, and tested planes, which included zooming down ten thousand feet in a steep dive. Pictures of the WASPs appeared in magazines such as *Life*, and newsreels of their work were shown in movie theaters.

By 1944 most Americans had come not only to accept but to cherish these women, so it was a shock when General

Arnold called in Jackie and ordered her to disband the WASP.

"But the war isn't over!" Jackie exclaimed.

"It's coming to an end. Fewer planes need to be delivered, and those that do can be flown by the Air Force men who are returning from Europe. The class scheduled to graduate in December will be the last class."

"What will I tell them?" Jackie had heard about women who'd been running farms throughout the war being told to leave the fields. Women in factories and offices were giving up their places at desks and machines to returning veterans. "They've taken orders from air force officers, flown air force planes, but they haven't even gotten military status. I can't send them home without veterans' pay or any medals. They deserve more."

General Arnold nodded, but he said there was nothing he could do.

Jackie wrote letters and spoke to some of the highest authorities in the military and Congress. It was a fight she lost. Many WASPs volunteered to work without pay, but their offers were turned down. One woman wrote to ask her family, "Can you use a good upstairs maid who has eight hundred flying hours?"

At the last WASP graduation, Jackie stood onstage next to Dedie Deaton, who'd helped arrange for thirty-eight funerals. She struggled to smile at the sixty-eight graduates who might never have another chance to fly.

General Arnold had agreed to be the speaker. "We will never again look upon a women's flying organization as experimental," he said. "We will know that women can handle our fastest fighters, our heaviest bombers; we will know that they are capable of ferrying, target towing, flying training, test flying, and countless other activities. We at the Army Air Force are proud of you. We will never forget our debt to you."

General Arnold pinned the WASP wings on lapels—silver wings with their center diamond-shaped, like the shield of Athena, goddess of courage and wisdom.

"It is on the record that women can fly as well as men," General Arnold said.

More than a thousand women had flown over sixty million miles for the Army Air Force. Others might forget what they'd done, but they would remember. As the women once known as WASPs packed lunches or stood in front of classrooms teaching history, their eyes sometimes strayed to windows. They would always remember how they had changed the sky.

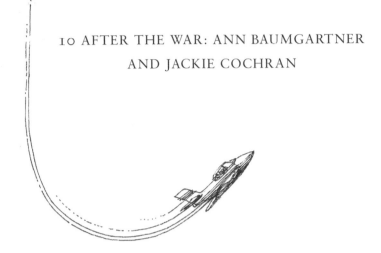

10 AFTER THE WAR: ANN BAUMGARTNER
AND JACKIE COCHRAN

fter the WASP disbanded, some women returned
to quiet lives in their hometowns, while others
found non-flying jobs in the military, ran flying
schools, became control tower operators, or fer-
ried civilian planes. No longer allowed to fly the air force
planes she'd been testing at Wright Field in Dayton, Ohio,
Ann Baumgartner took a job there writing public relations
material. At least she could stay near the planes and talk
about flying at dinner parties, where, as a young single
woman, she was often seated beside one of the few bachelors,
a gentleman in his seventies who wore a staid gray suit and
striking socks. He loved discussing the newest planes and jets,
but sometimes he spoke of how the black-topped airfield now

filled with silver planes had been a prairie when he was younger. He and his brother, Wilbur, had run through the grass beneath their wood-and-canvas *Flyer*.

One evening, Orville Wright asked Ann, "What kind of girl would want to fly military planes?"

What kind of girl? Ann had liked art, math, and science. Once she'd sat in the front row of her school's auditorium when Amelia Earhart, wearing a maroon dress with a white collar, had talked about a storm in the middle of the Atlantic, and how she'd wondered whether to keep going or turn around. Ann Baumgartner had gone to college, performed as a dancer, and worked as a scientist and a writer before enlisting in the WASP. She was assigned to Camp Davis, North Carolina, where she took the bed of a young librarian who'd died when the canopy of a burning plane wouldn't open.

Several months later, Ann and another woman were transferred to Wright Field to participate in medical research. After they'd helped assess some new equipment, Colonel Randy Lovelace encouraged Ann to apply for the flight testing division. She was the only woman accepted.

"I suppose you're like me," Orville Wright said to Ann. "You want to explore the unknown."

Ann piloted a wide variety of planes to try out new propellers or landing gear or anything that might make the plane faster and safer. She checked the progress of tests done to improve the planes used in combat. Sometimes she flew military personnel to other sites. She tested a high-altitude camera and shot guns over Lake Erie to try out a new gun sight. Ann was copilot of a B-29 Superfortress while trying to see if it could carry a nine-thousand-pound load, which was about the weight of a recently developed atomic bomb. Finally she became the first woman to fly a jet plane.

Within months, Ann, like all other WASPs, was barred from flying military planes. It would be nine years before another woman would pilot a jet. And it would take a woman with friends all over the country, especially in the Air Force. It would take a woman who didn't always play by the rules.

Jackie Cochran had a talent for finding new beginnings in what others saw as endings. Once the war was over, she spent more time with her husband and on her cosmetics business. She also decided to see more of the world. In Italy, she flew over Mount Vesuvius and saw the ruins of Pompeii. She met the Pope in Rome, watched ballet in Moscow, Russia, and attended the Nuremberg trials of Nazi war criminals in Germany. She traveled to India and saw the white marble walls of the Taj Mahal reflecting moonlight. She flew over vast deserts, lush rain forests, and icebergs in the Arctic Ocean.

Everywhere she met pilots, who talked about some of the changes the war had brought in aircraft. Jets drew in air that mixed with fuel, creating a force that burst out the back of the engines and hurled the plane forward. Chuck Yeager had flown a jet faster than the speed of sound.

Jackie wanted to do that, too, and spoke with military men. They reminded her that before reaching the speed she'd need to hit Mach one and break the sound barrier, the force of gravity would press down on her body, stressing her heart, lungs, and brain. The air pressure would change, which often

altered a pilot's perception. Many test pilots had died while trying to fly a jet so fast that the slightest move had turned them in the wrong direction.

"Jackie, you look great, but you're not young, and I heard your health isn't good," a general said. "A lot of men get up there, and once they're heading toward Earth, once they see the land getting awfully close, they pull back too soon. Or they freeze up and wait a second or two too long."

"I can do it," Jackie insisted.

"There are no second chances at that speed."

As director of the WASP, Jackie had risen to the rank of lieutenant colonel and been the first woman to earn the Distinguished Service Medal and the Distinguished Flying Cross. But she was not part of the military now, and she had to talk to dozens of people before finding some who were willing to let her go up in a jet.

Finally she strapped on a parachute, buckled herself into a seat, and adjusted the oxygen tank. She piloted the Sabrejet so high that the sky turned dark blue, then black. The engines made a high-pitched whine as she flew higher and higher, up about nine miles, beyond Earth's atmosphere, into space. She saw the stars at noon.

Then she turned the jet around. She had to be this high and head straight down in order to reach the speed necessary to break the sound barrier. Jackie didn't hesitate. She made the jet almost vertical and let out the throttle.

She flew faster than any woman had flown before.

Jackie was strapped in, but she was shaken by the intense vibration. Her legs throbbed as gravity pulled them down.

She sped toward the earth, where the heavier air could tear a plane apart. Moving at almost eight hundred miles an hour, she was going too fast to stop.

Then everything became quiet. The noise of the engine stopped. Her radio turned silent.

Jackie was flying so rapidly that sound waves couldn't move as fast as she was flying. For years she had flown with the racket of engines, and now that was gone.

Here I am, she thought as she shot through miles of sky. She turned the jet around at precisely the right moment. *Here I am.*

—

Soon after World War II ended, Ann Baumgartner married a pilot and engineer named Bill Carl. Ann Baumgartner Carl would always remember her adventures as a WASP, but before the war she'd held jobs as an artist, a dancer, a medical researcher, and a writer for The New York Times, *and she knew that life was full of opportunities for a person who looked ahead. Ann hoped to fly again someday (and she would), but meanwhile she had two children, enjoyed sailing, and wrote science articles for magazines and newspapers. Often she wrote about new developments in aviation. Jets were increasingly replacing airplanes that relied on propellers. Enormous computers were being built, and some people speculated that one day there would be computers small enough to put in planes to aid in navigation. Scientists experimenting with rockets spoke of the possibility of using their explosive power to break through the atmosphere into space.*

Jackie Cochran wondered about the future, too. After she broke the sound barrier and returned to earth to salutes, smiles, and hugs, she began planning ways to get back into the sky.

Through the following years, Jackie continued to test planes. But aircraft manufacturers needed publicity from broken speed and altitude records to sell planes, while newspaper editors worried that a picture of a plane and an aging woman—even one whose brown eyes still sparkled and whose hair was painstakingly coifed—wouldn't sell many papers. The flight news was tucked in the back pages of newspapers, and offers for Jackie to test planes became less frequent. And increasingly Jackie's health problems grew harder to ignore. She continued to fly at almost every opportunity, but sometimes she had to admit that a younger woman might do a better job.

Jackie enjoyed spending time with her husband, and she had plenty to think about. She remembered when it took days to cross the country in an airplane. Pilots had to stop often to refuel the small tanks, and because planes didn't have lights, pilots had to find fields to land on before dark. But back then, any woman who had enough money to take a few piloting lessons, or who was a good enough mechanic to fix a beat-up plane, or who had the guts to make a living by doing air stunts, could be a pilot. She might even buy her own plane.

Now heavy aircraft could go higher and faster than lighter, older planes. The sky seemed bigger and the world smaller than ever before. But most of the new, expensive jet planes were owned by the government and could be flown only by air force, army, or navy pilots. And ever since the WASPs had been sent home, the doors of military schools had stayed shut to women. There were a few women in the Air Force, but they weren't allowed to learn to pilot a jet plane.

As aircraft became more sophisticated, many thought the time for women pilots was over.

But Jackie Cochran was certain of one thing: women had piloted every kind of aircraft, and there was no reason that should change. As jets, rockets, and computers brought the world into an age of almost unimaginable speeds and heights, women would refuse to be left behind.

PART IV

HOW HIGH CAN WE GO? WOMEN IN SPACE
(1960–99)

Jerrie Cobb was twelve when her father gave her a ride in a small used airplane. From the sky, the Oklahoma prairies looked small. Horses galloped too slowly. The minute Jerrie and her father landed, she said, "I want to learn to fly."

Her father padded the cockpit seat with pillows so she could see out the window. He strapped blocks to the pedals so her legs could reach them. From the moment Jerrie took the controls, she knew she'd spend her life trying to go faster and higher.

In the little airport near her home, Jerrie lugged gasoline cans, washed airplanes, and handed tools to mechanics. By watching closely, she learned how to fix planes as well as how to fly them. At sixteen, she flew solo and earned her pilot's license.

After graduating from high school in 1948, Jerrie repaired an old plane and flew it across Texas, dropping leaflets to announce a circus. At night, farmers let her leave the plane in their fields. Jerrie spread her blankets under the wing and kept watch for cows, whose rough tongues could lick off the plane's paint. Her bed was hard, but no one had a better view of the moon.

When the circus closed, Jerrie took any job that would get her off the ground. She sprayed crops from the air. She flew low over oil fields to check pipes for leaks. When she was twenty-one, she applied for a pilot's job in Florida. The airport manager, who'd been impressed with the experience and ratings mentioned in her application, took one look at her and said, "Passengers are scared enough without seeing a girl in the cockpit."

Jerrie had spent her last dollar driving to Miami. She wasn't about to turn around. She took a job filing papers, consoling herself with the thought that she could look at planes before she was due at her desk each day.

Early one morning in 1953, she met a man who ran an air ferrying service. He complained that he couldn't find a pilot brave enough to fly a T-6 to South America. Jerrie opened her wallet to show him all her licenses.

"I'll give you a chance, just because I'm desperate," the man said, unfolding a map. He pointed to Jamaica, where Jerrie would stop for fuel. He drew his finger across the ocean to Peru. "The flight should take four hours. The tank holds

enough gas to last four hours and fifteen minutes. Be right or
be wet."

"When do you need this done?" Jerrie asked.

"I'll have the plane ready by sunrise tomorrow."

Jerrie was glad she was up early. She had almost twenty-
four hours to prepare.

Jerrie cleared her desk, quit her filing job, and rushed to
the library for books about the T-6 plane, which was more
powerful than any she'd flown. All night she studied the control panel. She put her folded parachute and life raft on the
seat so she could sit high enough to see through the window,
then set out just after dawn.

Jerrie kept the heavy plane on course through strong
winds. With only the sea below, she had to rely on instruments to tell if she was going the right way. She landed in Jamaica, filled her gas tank, and headed back to the sky. She
smiled as she spotted the coast, but she still had to make it
across the Andes, being careful of mountain peaks hidden behind clouds. Then she soared over miles of trees, where there
was no place to land if she ran out of fuel. Darkness came
suddenly near the equator. If the night caught her by surprise,
there would be no lights to guide her.

She landed the plane successfully just before dusk, and
spent the next few years delivering planes to air bases in Peru,
France, and India. Her home was in the cockpit or at air-
ports, where pilots argued about the chances of someone going into space.

The talk stirred Jerrie's dream of going still higher and
faster. She tested planes to see if they could withstand

high speeds and heights. Breaking an altitude record for a propeller-driven plane, she flew through the bluest sky she'd ever seen, up almost six miles, until the windshield became coated with ice.

By the time Jerrie was twenty-eight, she had been flying for sixteen years. She'd spent almost ten thousand hours in the air and set three world records for speed and altitude. At an air conference held in 1959, she met a doctor who was impressed with her accomplishments.

"I test planes for a living. I'm expected to break records," Jerrie said modestly. To change the subject, she asked, "Why don't you tell me what you do?"

"I specialize in flight medicine at NASA, the National Aeronautics and Space Administration, which was just founded," Dr. Randy Lovelace said.

"So it's true that people might go into space?" Jerrie looked up and tried to imagine the starry territory beyond the blue sky.

"Soon capsules with someone inside will be shot off rockets. The astronauts won't have room to wiggle their elbows or unbend their knees. I've been thinking about how most women are smaller and weigh less than men. They don't need as much food and oxygen. Every pound sent up will cost over a thousand dollars, so sending women into space could save money."

"I'd give anything for that chance!" Jerrie exclaimed.

"My job is to see who might be fit for space travel. Miss Cobb, the tests aren't easy or pleasant, and even if you pass, we can't promise that you'll be the first woman in space. And if you go up, no one can guarantee you'll get back."

"I've never asked for guarantees."

Not long afterward, Jerrie was invited to Dr. Lovelace's clinic, where he studied the way people might cope with changes in gravity and atmosphere. Dressed in full flight gear, Jerrie was plunged into water and had to escape from her test capsule. She was blasted into the air and spun around to see how she'd hold up when dizzy. She sat alone in a dark water tank for over nine hours to study the effects on her of isolation. Three feet of rubber tubing was crammed down her throat to test her capacity to withstand pain and nausea. Doctors examined her brain, eyes, ears, muscles, reflexes, and heart.

The results of all Jerrie's tests were outstanding. She met with Dr. Lovelace and his friend Jackie Cochran, now in her fifties, who was disappointed that her failing health kept her from qualifying for a new adventure.

"Women have been part of every sort of aviation. There's no reason for us to be left out of space," Jackie said. She asked her cosmetics company staff to look through files for the names of other highly experienced pilots, and she offered to pay the travel and lodging expenses of the women who came to test as astronauts.

Twelve other women passed the first set of rigorous tests. Gene Nora Stumbough Jessen, Myrtle Cagle, Wally Funk, Irene Leverton, and Bernice Steadman all made a living by teaching flying. Jerri Sloan Truhill worked for an aircraft company, demonstrating planes to possible buyers. Rhea Allison Woltman was a charter pilot. Jan Dietrich was a pilot for a construction company, and her twin, Marion, was a reporter who flew charter flights on weekends. Jean Hixson was a former WASP who still piloted when she wasn't teaching school. Sarah Lee Gorelick Ratley was an electrical engineer and commercial pilot. Jane Hart flew her husband, a senator, around when she wasn't looking after their eight children. Together the pilots became known as the Mercury 13.

Working as a NASA consultant, Jerrie spoke on radio and television to promote the space program. Reporters from *Time* magazine asked for her measurements. *Life* wanted to know if she could cook. "Badly," she replied. In front of television cameras, she tried to smile at comments on her trim figure and blond ponytail and questions such as, "Why isn't a pretty girl like you married? Are you more afraid of men than space?"

Further testing and training was scheduled at the Naval Air Station in Pensacola, Florida. Then, two days before the program was to begin, Jerrie got a phone call from Dr. Lovelace. He told her that the testing had been canceled. All plans for women in the space program were off.

The women who'd left their homes returned. Those who'd quit jobs began to look for other work. But Jerrie headed to Washington, D.C., where she was told, "NASA staff can't spare the time, which is needed for training men. We can't afford to buy new equipment, such as smaller, slightly different space suits."

"NASA just got three billion dollars from the govern-

ment," Jerrie said. "You can afford to make an extra space suit or two."

"This isn't the right time," one NASA official replied. "President Kennedy just promised to get a man on the moon by 1970. That's a lot of work to do in less than ten years."

Jerrie Cobb left the office, but she continued to write letters and make phone calls to anyone she thought might help give the Mercury 13 another chance. She traveled around the country giving speeches. "The Russians beat us into space," she said. "They sent a man into orbit before we did. But we can be the first to send a woman into space."

As a representative for the Fédération Aéronautique Internationale, Jerrie went to Cape Canaveral to watch a towering rocket blast off and launch a space capsule. People had brought radios and televisions into schools and workplaces around the country to learn the news when John Glenn became the first American to orbit the earth, in 1962.

Shortly after the blond, blue-eyed astronaut was welcomed back with parades and parties, Jerrie got a call from Jane Hart, one of the Mercury 13 who was familiar with politics because of her husband's work in the Senate. She suggested that they take their fight for equal treatment beyond the halls of NASA to Capitol Hill.

Nine congressmen and two congresswomen agreed to meet with Jerrie and Jane and NASA representatives at a hearing.

"There were women on the *Mayflower* and on the first wagon trains going West, working alongside the men. We ask for that opportunity in the pioneering of space," Jerrie said. She kept her eyes away from John Glenn and Scott Carpenter, astronauts who'd come to testify for NASA.

"We are not suggesting that women be admitted to space merely so that we won't feel discriminated against," Jane Hart said. "We are asking to be admitted because we have a very real contribution to make. Too many of our citizens are behind those of other countries in their knowledge of math and science. Leaving women out of the space program gives half our children the message that they shouldn't bother with science."

Some congressmen agreed with the women. But more nodded when John Glenn said, "The fact that women are not in this field is a fact of our social order."

Cameras clicked as reporters elbowed one another to get a better shot of the famous astronaut. The hall boomed with laughter at John Glenn's jokes about what might happen if women went into space.

Jerrie Cobb and Jane Hart struggled to turn the hall serious again. "Scientists have shown that women seem to withstand loneliness, boredom, and isolation better," Jerrie said. "They can tolerate extremes of heat, cold, and pain."

The NASA representatives said it was necessary for all astronauts to have experience testing jet planes.

"The only way to get that experience is through the Air Force, which doesn't accept women in its schools," Jerrie argued. "The women of the Mercury 13 have an average of 4,500 hours in the air, a higher average of flying hours than the male astronaut candidates have. No one spends that much time in the air without coping with emergencies that call for split-second reactions."

John Glenn argued that no number of hours could make up for experience in a jet.

Jerrie disagreed. "What counts is flawless judgment, fast reaction, and the ability to transmit this to the proper control of the craft."

A congressman from Pennsylvania suggested that NASA's apparent desire to protect women only kept them from opportunities for adventure enjoyed by men. He asked John Glenn if he would oppose a training program for women.

"I wouldn't oppose it," John Glenn replied. He added, "I see no requirement for it."

As if that opinion could not be argued, the hearing ended. Congressmen and reporters crowded around John Glenn and Scott Carpenter to ask for autographs. Nothing had been decided, and Jerrie was hopeful, but it soon became clear that public admiration for the astronauts overshadowed everything that she and her supporters had said.

Jerrie's contract with NASA was not renewed. She kept fighting, but more and more of her letters went unanswered. Phone calls were not returned. Jerrie grieved, but as Jackie Cochran had done when the WASP was disbanded, she looked for a new beginning in an ending.

Jerrie found church groups who wanted to donate food and medical supplies to people in the Amazon rain forest. She saved money to buy a small plane she called *Juliet*, and headed back to the wide skies of South America. The plane was as small and almost as dilapidated as the one on which she'd first learned to pilot twenty years before. Alone in the plane, soaring over vast forests, she thought she might be in more danger than she would have been in, in space. She drew her own maps and ventured into villages where people had no word for "plane," since they'd never seen one. No one cared whether it was a man or a woman who brought the food and medicine that was needed.

Jerrie had been in the Amazon for less than a year when she heard over her radio that a Russian woman had flown into space, on June 16, 1963. Valentina Tereshkova had grown up on a farm, worked in a factory, joined a sky-diving club, and learned to fly a plane. She sang in the space capsule as it circled the earth for seventy-one hours, or more time than all the American astronauts put together had spent in space.

Jerrie played tag with the clouds in celebration, though she couldn't help wishing that the first woman in space had been an American. She couldn't help wishing that it had been she. She was grateful for her new life in the rain forest. She loved watching parrots and toucans dart above flowers no one else could see. But she didn't plan to stay away from her old home forever. When the time came to send an American woman pilot into space, she wanted to be there.

A few months after Valentina Tereshkova's safe return to Earth, news of President John F. Kennedy's assassination came over Jerrie's radio. She mourned the dreamer who'd hoped to see an astronaut on the moon by the end of the 1960s, and she grieved for the practical man who, shortly before he died, urged Americans and Russians to consider the money that could be saved and the peace that might be created if our nations worked together to reach the moon, instead of racing to be first.

During the next six years, Jerrie kept flying over thick forests, transporting farming supplies, and sleeping in a hammock. She didn't pay much attention to most of the reports from North America broadcast over her radio. But one day in 1969, while she was in the air, some news made her cheer and play with the clouds again.

She followed a river to a creek that marked the way to an airstrip she'd recently helped clear. She landed, and men with painted faces unloaded bags of bean seeds and small papaya trees. Jerrie lifted children onto the plane's tail to make it heavier. Then, with the front wheel in the air, she and some men turned the plane so that it faced the runway. Many hands passed buckets to refuel.

Only when *Juliet* was ready to take off the next morning did Jerrie say, "I heard that yesterday a spaceship landed on the moon!"

A few people nodded politely, but no one seemed excited. So Jerrie pointed to the pale, rising moon and added, "Someone could be walking there right now!"

Her friends turned to one another and began talking about supper. "Come. Have some soup," a woman said.

Jerrie thanked her, but shook her head. People headed back to the big hut. As Jerrie was hanging her hammock under the wing of her plane, the shaman said, "Our ancestor, Birdman, has been to the moon many times."

Jerrie said good night. She climbed onto the wing of her

plane, stood on her toes, breathed the scents of ferns and leaves, and raised her arms.

To the music of wind in the trees, she danced across the wings.

—

Millions of Americans had gathered in front of televisions to watch Neil Armstrong touch the moon's cratered surface. President John F. Kennedy had died six years before, but his words were remembered: "We choose to go to the moon in this decade, and to do all the other things, not because they are easy, but because they are hard."

Some people believed the televised moon landing was a hoax created by special effects. Others thought the space flights were a waste of money better spent on improving life on Earth. Most people were briefly amazed by photographs of the stark moon and the earth, which looked round and blue-and-white from space, then returned to whatever they'd been doing before. Jerrie Cobb went back to the work she would continue as long as there were bean seeds to deliver and people who needed a lift to reach the medical care their shamans couldn't provide.

For some girls, the moon launch shaped dreams that changed their lives.

Shannon Wells was born in China to missionary parents. Since her family returned to the United States to visit relatives every few years, by the time Shannon was six years old, she had traveled around the world twice. After the family settled in Oklahoma, her mother told Shannon that when it was night there, it was daytime back in China. When it was noon at home, people on the other side of the world were sleeping. The young scientist refused to believe what she hadn't seen with her own eyes. She set off down the sidewalk, pulling a small red wagon behind her.

Some grownups asked her where she was going. "I want to explore the world," she said.

For a while, Shannon had to be content with chasing the tumbleweeds that blew across the prairies. As she grew older, she read science fiction about beings who traveled between planets in remarkable vehicles. She loved to speed around town, but she sold her bicycle to buy a telescope, which seemed to take her places, too. She marveled at the pictures she saw in magazines of the first astronauts, though there was something about the pictures of men in silver suits and helmets that made her uneasy. Shannon wrote a letter to Time, asking, "Where are the women?"

She never got an answer, but some questions are as important as replies. In the early 1970s, more and more people questioned why newspapers advertised jobs for women separately from jobs open to men, which were often more challenging and better paid. Women began fighting for opportunities to train for work fixing machines, building houses, and changing laws. They demanded equal rights and pay in sports, on the stage, and above the earth.

In 1977, the Air Force opened its flight schools to women and released the statement: "For the first time, the Air Force is allowing women to fly its aircraft."

Women rejoiced, for the only way most people could

learn to pilot an expensive and complex jet was by joining the military. But after the celebrations, some took a closer look at the announcement from the Air Force.

"For the first time? What about us?" the women who'd been WASPs asked.

They had accepted low pay to serve their country during World War II. For thirty years, they had received no veterans' benefits. They didn't expect money or awards now, but they refused to be written out of history.

Over eight hundred WASPs sent letters asking for the simple recognition that they had flown planes for the Air Force. Their protest was backed by every woman member of Congress. Bruce Arnold, the son of General Hap Arnold, who'd directed the Army Air Force during World War II, supported them as he believed his father would have done if he were still alive. Jackie Cochran was now in her seventies and too ill to travel, but other WASPs went to Washington, D.C., with letters, photographs, and documents proving an existence that too many had forgotten.

On November 3, 1977, the House of Representatives unanimously passed a bill, which the Senate quickly approved. Thirty-three years after the WASPs were sent home, President Jimmy Carter signed a paper honoring them with official military recognition.

Since eighth grade, when Shannon Wells studied rockets for her science project, she did everything she could to be ready in case NASA opened its programs to women. She cleaned houses to earn money for flying lessons and took lots of science courses in college. She earned an advanced degree in biochemistry and found a job doing medical research.

One Saturday, when it was too rainy to fly, Shannon accepted a date from a colleague. After she and Michael Lucid married, she became known as Dr. Shannon Wells Lucid.

The couple started a family. When her first baby was a few weeks old, Shannon powdered her, kissed her, and made sure she was snug beside her in the cockpit. Her next two babies

got rides, too. She wanted her children to get used to the hum
and roar of engines, to know that there was more to life than
the earth and more to her than the person who fed and held
them. Their mother was a pilot, and the sky was going to be
a big part of their lives.

In 1978 NASA, acting in compliance with the new antidis-
crimination laws, advertised for women candidates. The
cramped Mercury and Apollo capsules, which had carried
John Glenn around the earth and Neil Armstrong to the
moon, were being replaced with larger shuttles that would
carry teams of five to eight people. While experienced jet pilots would continue to be commanders of these space shuttles, NASA decided that not all astronauts needed to be test
pilots. They wanted to have scientists, whom they would call
mission specialists, aboard.

Jerrie Cobb, who was still flying in the Amazon rain
forests, heard about the new opportunities at NASA, but she
was too old to meet the physical requirements, and she didn't
have the necessary years in college. Besides, she had other
challenges now. Younger people, such as Shannon Lucid,
competed with about one thousand women and six thousand
men for thirty-five positions. Many applicants had strong
backgrounds in astronomy and physics. There were doctors
of medicine who planned to study how the lack of gravity
and other conditions of space and speed affected humans.
Geologists wanted to discover new things about the earth by
seeing it from far above, while engineers would work on ways
to improve the spacecraft.

After months of interviews and tests, Shannon Lucid,

Kathryn Sullivan, Sally Ride, Anna Fisher, Margaret Rhea Seddon, and Judith Resnik were selected as mission specialists. These six women often worked together and suggested the few changes their gender made necessary: a uniform of pants and shirt rather than a jumpsuit would make it easier for them to use the spacecraft's suction-style toilet. The shuttle seats were rebuilt to adjust for legs of varying lengths.

The women's training was identical to the men's, but reporters insisted on taking pictures of them as a group. Trips to space had become old news, but here was a new story: who would be the first American woman to fly into space?

Smiling at reporters became part of the women's job. The expensive space programs depended on taxpayers' money, so upbeat articles and news clips helped ensure that Americans would continue to support NASA programs. Shannon and the other women told reporters about their ongoing study of science, but reporters seemed to care only about the novelty of their being women.

"Dr. Lucid, what will you tell your children if you go up in space?" they asked.

Shannon, who was usually easygoing, couldn't keep a bit of irritation from her voice as she replied, "I won't be the first parent to go into space. Why don't you ask the astronauts who are dads what their kids think?"

Shannon was glad to get back to studying navigation, weather, and every electrical wire and circuit of the shuttle. She trained in simulators that were like the shuttles. She practiced swimming underwater wearing scuba gear, since that was the closest feeling to life in zero gravity.

The mission specialists piloted jets and studied the shuttle's control boards so they'd know what to do if something happened to the shuttle pilot or commander. They leaped from planes and opened parachutes. To prepare for the possibility of landing in the ocean, the trainees swam while hauling equipment. Everyone learned how to weave fishnets from string and how to turn their parachutes into tents in case they ended up on a remote island.

No one knew what criteria would be used to choose the first woman to go into space, but working and studying together, the six women were more friendly than competitive. Shannon found that Kathy Sullivan had grown up on a farm, where she used to sit on the barn roof and wonder about the skies. She'd trained as a geologist and loved working with a hammer and chisel to discover the history hidden in rocks.

Sally Ride was twenty-six years old. A perfectionist on the tennis court and in classrooms, she'd majored in both English and physics in college, and had earned a doctorate degree in astrophysics by investigating the X rays given off by stars. Judy Resnik was an electrical engineer who was crazy about chocolate and played the piano with finesse. Two of the women were medical doctors. Anna Fisher had been called a tomboy as a girl because she liked playing football with her three brothers, but she also enjoyed demonstrating her grace and strength doing ballet. Margaret Rhea Seddon was a surgeon. Since she went by her middle name, which was pronounced "ray," she was often called "Cosmic Rhea."

After several years of training, Sally Ride was chosen as the first American woman to go into space. Reporters trailed

her to ask, "How does it feel to be the first American woman going into space?" and "Do you cry when something goes wrong?" Sally's smile got tighter as she tried to get back to work. As the flight engineer, her job would be to make sure that all instruments were working properly and to help release two communications satellites.

Finally, in 1983, everything was ready for the launch. Shannon and her friends gathered around a television to watch. Cameras swept the cheering crowds at the Kennedy Space Center, Cape Canaveral, where girls waved posters that read, "Ride, Sally, Ride!" Sally was smiling in the slightly impatient way Shannon recognized. She cared more about space and science than applause, but she was making history whether she wanted to or not. As the shuttle lifted off, girls who were fascinated by rockets, as Shannon had been, girls who looked through telescopes, girls who loved fast horses, bicycles, and sleds, could imagine themselves in the sky.

A year after Sally Ride and the rest of the crew returned safely, Judy Resnik was chosen to go into space, becoming the first Jewish astronaut. A friend baked her brownies, which she smuggled aboard and ate for breakfast. In 1984 Sally Ride went up again, along with Kathy Sullivan, who became the first American woman to walk in space. Rhea Seddon went up the following year. NASA officials told Anna Fisher she'd be next.

Shannon continued to train, but it sometimes seemed that her days were filled with either packing her children's lunches and sending them off to school or waving to friends before they blasted into space. She knew that astronauts had to learn to say a cheerful goodbye to friends headed where they wished to go, but she couldn't help wondering if she'd ever get a turn.

Finally, Shannon began to prepare to work on a shuttle deploying equipment to take pictures of the billions of stars in the Milky Way. Seven years after she joined NASA, Shannon hugged her husband and three children goodbye. She looked up at the tall, silver shuttle. Fuel had been pumped into *Discovery* for hours, and now it shook and looked almost alive as vapor puffed from the top.

Shannon waved to reporters as she headed toward the shuttle. Technicians helped her into the big, clumsy suit everyone wore during liftoff. Shannon slipped into a seat with her back parallel to the ground, her face toward the sky, her knees bent against her chest. She snapped on her seat belt, checked her oxygen hose and radio, then watched sea gulls soar and swoop over the marshes around Cape Canaveral.

The hours, minutes, and seconds until the spacecraft would lift off were regularly announced, using terms from rocket science: T − 1 hour, which was read as "T minus one hour," meant there were sixty minutes before the shuttle was scheduled to leave the earth.

The countdown changed from minutes to seconds. "T − 10. T − 9 . . ."

Shannon's heart beat hard as she thought of all the people there in Florida and at the Johnson Space Center in Houston, Texas, who were hunched intently over monitors, making sure the many complex systems were working.

"T − 8. T − 7. T − 6 . . ."

At T − 6 Shannon felt the shuttle shake harder as, one after another, the engines ignited. Then the shuttle blasted off the earth. Shannon could see the whole space center in a glance, then most of Florida, then a long strip of coast. Within a minute, they were flying faster than the speed of sound. The force of gravity made it difficult to lift her arms.

Only six minutes after liftoff, *Discovery* was in orbit, traveling around the earth at 17,500 miles per hour, or thirty times the speed of most jets. Shannon took off her gloves and helmet, which began to float. The crew grabbed one another's equipment to fasten down with bungee cords, Velcro, and duct tape. Without gravity, Shannon's body had no sense of its weight. Her legs drifted one way, her arms another. Everyone climbed out of bulky space suits to reveal the T-shirts and shorts worn while in space.

Shannon floated toward the window to look at the blue, green, and brown world. Entire countries could be seen in one glance. The lovely curve of the earth was visible. Overhead and all around her, space loomed. Shannon smiled, then turned from the window. She wasn't here to gaze and wonder at the darkness brightened by stars. There was work to do.

—

Rocketing past the force of gravity to fly at tremendous speeds always poses great risks, but through the first half of the 1980s, space shuttles flew with a regularity that most Americans found humdrum. Launches were rarely televised, and reports of safe returns were kept to a few lines in the back pages of newspapers. As more and more people began to think that space flights were a waste of taxpayers' money, some NASA staff decided to build enthusiasm for its programs by sending an ordinary citizen into space, a schoolteacher rather than a highly trained astronaut.

Christa McAuliffe, a history teacher from New Hampshire, was chosen from among more than eleven thousand applicants. NASA administrators hoped that this woman with brown eyes and a bubbly voice could convey her enthusiasm for space exploration to classrooms and homes across the country. Other applicants had submitted complicated plans, but Christa proposed simply to keep a journal. She believed that a diary, like those kept by settlers in journeys in covered wagons, could reveal the hardships and wonder of space travel. Christa also planned to give videotaped lessons from space, beginning with one titled "The Ultimate Field Trip."

Some of the astronauts, who'd spent years preparing for work in space that they'd have to do in the span of a few days, were afraid Christa would get in their way. But as the energetic teacher spent months training, the astronauts were won over by her respect for them, her curiosity about their work, and her sincere wish to be helpful. Christa's new friends showed her around Houston, and she was often invited to join the astronauts for supper at their favorite restaurant, where she exchanged jokes with Judy Resnik and asked Ronald McNair about his children, before telling stories about her little girl and boy.

The flight of Christa McAuliffe, Commander Francis Scobee, pilot Michael Smith, and mission specialists Gregory

Jarvis, Ronald McNair, Ellison Onizuka, and Judith Resnik captured the attention of people who hadn't watched a televised launch in years. The team included an African American man, an Asian man, and a Jewish woman, reflecting the nation's diversity.

The well-publicized launch was delayed for weeks because of problems with the spacecraft, then bad weather. Finally, on January 28, 1986, everyone at the Johnson Space Center who wasn't directly involved in the launch gathered in front of television screens. As the countdown began, Shannon Lucid remembered the excitement of her own space flight seven months before.

People crowded around the television to count along with the announcer. Everyone cheered as he said, "It's a liftoff!"

For half a minute, the shuttle rose. It twisted and leveled out to follow the earth's curve. Then, seventy-three seconds after it left the earth, a terrible light flashed.

Instead of flying out of sight, merging into the sky, the shuttle disappeared in clouds of gray smoke. More smoke fell in trails.

The announcer quietly said, "Obviously, a major malfunction."

The words echoed. No one could speak. It was hard even to breathe. Shannon and her friends huddled together to watch, over and over, shots of the liftoff. She felt caught in the desperate hope that if she watched long enough, the ending might change.

But Challenger *had exploded. High above the earth, seven people had died.*

Shannon went home, where her children stared at the tel-evised image of the short flight, the sky marked by smoke. Shannon's youngest child, her son, turned to her for comfort, but one of her teenaged daughters screamed, "Don't astro-nauts think about anyone but themselves? Don't they care about their children?"

Shannon let her daughter yell. She watched the image of smoke blooming and falling as she thought that she'd never again see Ron McNair with his baby girl, her black hair twisted in dozens of braids, bouncing on his shoulders. Hous-ton wouldn't be the same. She wouldn't see Ellison Onizuka drive his kids to soccer practice, or hear them slam the car door and yell, "Bye, Dad!" Judy Resnik would never again play the piano, eat a brownie for breakfast, or crack another joke.

"What will Christa McAuliffe's husband tell their little boy and girl?" Shannon's daughter asked.

Shannon shook her head. She didn't know.

"Will you go up again, Mom?" one of her children asked.

"NASA won't send up anyone until they're convinced the flight is safe," Shannon said.

She would never forget her friends who had died above the earth, but if she ever got another chance to fly into space, she wouldn't turn it down. She couldn't think of a single as-tronaut who would.

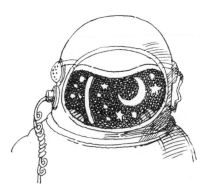

Eileen Collins had just returned from testing air force jets when she got a phone call from NASA. If she was still interested, she could become the first woman to train to pilot a space shuttle.

Eileen had dreamed about becoming an astronaut since she was a girl and crowded among her father, brothers, and sister on the hood of their car, watching gliders swoop above the local airfield. Eileen saw her father's face turn peaceful as he briefly forgot his job, which didn't pay enough to get the family out of public housing or off food stamps.

Eileen's brothers and sister quickly grew restless and begged their dad to take them out for ice cream, but Eileen could watch the gliders for a long, long time, intrigued with what looked graceful and easy, but took practice, knowledge, and courage. She asked her father how the pilots knew when the winds might shift direction and how it was possible for something heavier than air to hang suspended. He couldn't answer all her questions, but he drove her to the library, where she found books about weather, the physics and mechanics of flight, the planes used in Vietnam and earlier wars, and the stories of Amelia Earhart, Bessie Coleman, and Jackie Cochran.

These were the women who kept Eileen company as she worked at a pizza shop to pay for flying lessons and college. She earned a college degree in mathematics, then became one of four women in an air force pilot training program.

In 1978, many of the teachers who'd spent their entire careers working with men ignored or insulted the new women students. Some male students stared at Eileen as if they couldn't believe she could fly a military jet. A few hinted that she must have met easier standards than they had to get into the Air Force.

Eileen learned to shrug off the insults. She completed her military training and became the only woman in a squadron of one hundred pilots, flying troops and cargo to air bases around the world. She trained novice pilots and kept taking classes in order to learn to fly a wide variety of aircraft.

She'd begun testing jet planes, and had recently married pilot Pat Youngs, when she got the call from NASA asking her to start astronaut training. Whenever Eileen had imagined that day, she thought she'd shriek and shout and race around the room. Instead, she quietly put down the phone and began making plans with Pat to move to Houston. After all, she was a highly experienced pilot, used to being thrilled and calm at the same time.

During the next five years, Eileen trained on simulators, learning how to monitor the shuttle's main engines and electrical systems. In 1995 she was scheduled to pilot *Discovery*. The shuttle's most important mission would be to see if it could safely approach the Russian space station, *Mir*. If Eileen helped prove that the shuttle could dock with the space station, an American astronaut might join the Russians aboard it. Two American astronauts were already at Star City, Russia's astronaut training center, preparing to fly aboard *Mir*.

Eileen practiced using radar guns and other sensor systems that would help her determine distances as she steered the shuttle toward the space station. There would be no surrounding objects to help determine *Mir*'s location amid vast black space. Eileen and Commander James Wetherbee would have to pilot the shuttle at just the right speed, then align it with the rings of *Mir*'s docking area so precisely that if they made an error of more than an inch, the mission would fail.

Human lives and millions of dollars' worth of equipment would be in Eileen's hands. She knew that if anyone thought she'd made even a slight error in judgment, she might never pilot another shuttle. And there were people likely to think that if one woman made a mistake, no woman pilot could be trusted.

Eileen prepared for every sort of emergency and kept training. She thought about how she hadn't gotten to the pilot's seat of a spacecraft by herself. Other women had given her courage along the way. Except in books, she'd never met most of her heroes. Many had died before she was born, but that didn't matter. None was forgotten.

Shortly before she was scheduled to take off, Eileen located a scarf that had belonged to Amelia Earhart to bring with her aboard the shuttle. Jackie Cochran had died, but Eileen invited some WASPs to see her launch, and she borrowed their silver wings for luck. She discovered that Jerrie Cobb had spent most of the past thirty years flying in South America. Maybe that was too far for her to come to a launch that would be over in minutes. Maybe Jerrie's struggle for a woman's right to pilot a spacecraft had taken place too long ago.

But Eileen wanted to find her.

—

Jerrie Cobb stood in the bleachers at the Kennedy Space Center, along with six other pilots who'd been part of the Mercury 13. Jerrie looked at the dark sky and the lights around the tall silver shuttle. The roar of rockets made it difficult to talk, though hundreds of people cheered as the countdown began. Warm, salty breezes wafted off the ocean.

A brilliant flash of light was followed by thundering noise. The earth shook even in the bleachers, which were a few miles from the launchpad. Jerrie bent back her neck to follow the trail of fire and smoke. She was happy with her life, flying her own plane, helping people in remote regions of Ecuador, Peru, and Brazil, but she couldn't help wishing, even now, that she was in that shuttle.

Go, go, *Jerrie thought as Eileen Collins piloted* Discovery *into the sky. She carried a golden pin shaped like a condor, a beautiful, endangered bird, that had been a gift from Jerrie. She carried the courage and dreams of the women who came before her, and the dreams of girls who were bound to follow.*

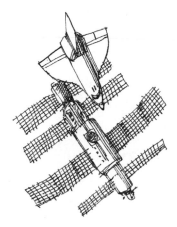

Cosmonauts at Star City anxiously listened to satellite reports as they followed *Discovery*'s progress in 1995. This would be the first time in twenty years that Americans and Russians met in space, and the first time a shuttle had been piloted to *Mir*. The shuttles the Russians sent to *Mir* had always been directed by people operating computers on earth. The Russians thought that guiding a spacecraft from Mission Control was safer than relying on astronauts' piloting skills.

"Commander Jim Wetherbee and Pilot Eileen Collins will do great," Shannon Lucid assured everyone. She had come to Star City in Moscow a few months before to prepare for work aboard *Mir*. At fifty-four, Shannon had flown into space four times. Working in a laboratory aboard a space station seemed like the perfect job for a scientist and a pilot like herself. But now she worried that even a minor problem might make the Russians ask her and other Americans to go home.

During the first twenty-four hours of *Discovery*'s three-day flight, Shannon tried to concentrate on her work at Star City. As usual, she got up at five and went to bed at midnight, after poring over engineering and chemistry books written in Russian. On the second day of *Discovery*'s flight, news reached Russia that the shuttle had developed a small fuel leak. NASA determined that there would be enough fuel to continue, though there would be none available to correct a mistake. As the astronauts prepared to dock with *Mir*, they would not get a second chance to turn or back up or approach again. Even worse news was that the drops of fuel spewing out were turning into icy crystals. The Russians worried that these crystals could strike *Mir* and damage its sensitive equipment.

Shannon was glad to hear that NASA staff were flying to Star City with models, graphs, and charts to demonstrate that the excess fuel would be gone by the time the shuttle reached the space station. After hours of questions and arguments, the Russians agreed that the attempt to rendezvous in space could continue.

As *Discovery* flew closer to *Mir*, Shannon Lucid and her colleagues crowded around the radio to listen as Commander Jim Wetherbee and Pilot Eileen Collins worked boosters, brakes, and control thrusts. Both spacecraft weighed more than one hundred tons. Both moved at 17,500 miles per hour.

If *Discovery* came in even a little too fast, the collision might prove fatal. But if it moved too slowly, the mechanisms designed to hitch the vehicles wouldn't work.

Discovery glided up to *Mir* perfectly.

Commander Jim Wetherbee's voice came over the radio. "As we bring our spacecraft together, we are bringing our nations together."

The commander of *Mir* cried, "We are all one! We are all human!"

Shannon threw up her arms with joy.

Through the following months, she continued to work six days a week, taking off Sundays to bicycle in the forests or tour Moscow museums. She'd prepared twenty-eight experiments by the time a shuttle was ready to take her on the three-day journey to *Mir*. Halfway there, she thought the space station sparkled like a distant star. As they got closer, Shannon studied the cluster of five modules with solar panels jutting every which way. *Mir* reminded her of the tumbleweeds she'd chased while growing up in Oklahoma, though, of course, the space station was larger and whirled through space instead of over prairies.

The shuttle and space station thudded smoothly together. Then Shannon kicked and waved her arms like a swimmer to float into the main module. It smelled like dirty sneakers in a gas station. Air circulators and hundreds of other machines buzzed. Pipes and tangled wires were exposed. Clipboards, laptop computers, and cases of videotapes were Velcroed to surfaces to keep them from bobbing around.

Yuri Onufriyenko and Yuri Usachev greeted Shannon with

the traditional Russian gift of bread and salt. Shannon gave them some oranges, a fragrant treat for cosmonauts whose meals came out of foil packets. The two men then turned back to the control panels that covered most of one wall. They spread their arms over the dials and levers, as if they thought Shannon might dart forward and try to take over. She reminded herself that friendships take time. Russians and Americans had grown up wondering if the others' country would start a nuclear war with them. She remembered the drills at school, with kids ducking under desks as if that might keep them safe from nuclear bombs.

Living with strangers in a crowded space might not be easy, but Shannon had planned experiments that could be done only in these conditions of near-zero gravity. And what she learned aboard this space station would be used to help build the International Space Station.

Since the most dangerous parts of shuttle missions were the liftoffs and landings, many people thought that rather than continually sending up shuttles, it would be safer and less expensive to keep a space station orbiting the earth. Experiments could be run for long periods, instead of the five to ten days that most shuttle trips lasted. Telescopes and satellites could be repaired, even built, aboard a space station, and they could be launched from there. Individual countries didn't have the resources to build such a great project alone, but they could do it together, saving time and money by not duplicating one another's efforts.

Shannon was determined to make these five small, cluttered modules into a home. If three people couldn't get along up here, how could people from sixteen countries work together to build the International Space Station? She looked down at the earth, where lines didn't divide countries the way they did on maps, and reminded herself that the Russian word *Mir* meant "peace."

Shannon left Base Block, which contained the main control board, a dining area, and two curtained-off sleeping areas for the Russian cosmonauts. She floated through a passageway and peered into a module used for storing trash and supplies. Another module held a shower and a toilet, and there was a slightly larger one where experiments were set up. She strapped her sleeping bag to the wall in the fifth module, called Spektr, then hung up cartons to hold her books and tapes.

She floated back to Base Block, where she and Yuri Onufriyenko and Yuri Usachev added water to foil packets, kneading them to make a supper of beet soup and potato casserole. Later, she belted herself into her sleeping bag.

The next morning, Shannon woke up in about the same place where she'd gone to sleep. Yuri and Yuri were busy repairing the ten-year-old space station, which had been built to last about five years. The Russian air force commander and the engineer diagnosed problems and fixed coolant leaks and Elektron breakdowns, while Shannon set up some of the twenty-eight experiments she'd planned. She planted wheat in a small greenhouse to study plant growth in zero gravity. She prepared a study to see how embryos developed in quail eggs, and another to observe how metals heated and cooled in space.

As the weeks passed, Shannon felt as if she were stuck in a crowded camper through day after day of rain. But she kept on with her science and worked out on the treadmill for two hours every day. She chose a tape, put on her headset, and attached a harness to hold down her body. She pulled on stretchy cords that resisted her effort, the way gravity would on earth. She walked for longer than it took *Mir* to orbit the earth. While she enjoyed the view of many more stars than could be seen from below, two hours of walking in place got boring. But Shannon wanted to prove that life in space didn't have to harm one's health. Since there was no gravity to push against, muscles became weak from lack of use. Most people who returned from more than a few weeks in space had to be carried off on a stretcher. Shannon hoped that if she exercised regularly, she'd stay fit enough to walk off the shuttle without help.

Circling the earth, Shannon could see the sun rise and set sixteen times in twenty-four hours, so the astronauts followed a clock set to Moscow time. While Shannon strapped herself into her sleeping bag, she thought of her family back in Texas, who were just getting out of beds that remained on the floor. When they swung their feet down, their legs stayed beneath them. They picked up cups that didn't float and poured milk that fell predictably, gracefully down. Shannon missed her family, but she became friends with the men she called "the two Yuris." They traded packets of beet soup for packets of mayonnaise and tossed Shannon's M&M's across the table to one another. The green, red, and yellow candies bobbed between them as they talked about growing up when their countries were enemies, and how far they had come.

Almost every evening, Shannon e-mailed her husband and her children, who were grown now and busy with jobs or college. They wrote about problems with their cars or classes, and her older daughter sent Shannon thick novels on a shuttle delivery flight. While Shannon had loved science fiction as a girl, now that she was in space she enjoyed books written by people who'd lived before the Wright brothers. She treasured Charles Dickens's descriptions of the scent of bread baking over wood, the sounds of china teacups settling into saucers, and horses clip-clopping on cobblestone streets.

Sometimes she took pictures for scientists on earth who studied weather, oceans, or geology. Sometimes she simply stared at her favorite planet, where she could see entire countries in one glance. It was easy to spot the long peninsula of Florida, the hook of Cape Cod in Massachusetts, and Italy, shaped like a boot. When *Mir* orbited closer to the earth, she could make out highways, rivers, and bridges. She spotted the Pyramids in Egypt, fires raging through forests, and erupting volcanoes. When it was dark on Earth, clusters of lights marked the cities along the California coast. Lights glittered around the edges of the Great Lakes and the Gulf of Mexico. Soon she could look down on the Eastern Seaboard, where Boston, New York, Philadelphia, and Washington, D.C., were marked by glowing lights.

After about six months in space, Shannon said goodbye to the cosmonauts and rode the shuttle back to Earth. Her legs felt wobbly as she put her weight on them. Her stride wasn't elegant—it was a sort of shuffle—but she passed men waiting with stretchers and walked down the corridor on her own. Her husband and children hugged her. President Bill Clinton came to offer congratulations on a very successful trip.

It was lovely to stand without her feet floating up, and to move in a straight line instead of circles. She enjoyed lifting her elbows without worrying that they would bump into something the way they did in the crowded modules. The fresh air smelled fantastic. In her 188 days in space, Shannon had gone around the earth three thousand times, breaking the American record for the most time spent in space. She smiled and shook hands and confided that she looked forward to a long, hot shower. But she couldn't help glancing at the sky that had been her home for a long time. She couldn't help wondering when she'd go back.

—

While Shannon Lucid orbited the earth in Mir, *and after she returned, Donna Shirley drove to work in her Saturn car with its license plate that read "Mars." Donna Shirley had grown up reading science fiction and watching* Star Trek. *She earned her pilot's license at sixteen, studied aerospace engineering in college, and eventually became the first woman to manage a NASA program, heading a team of thirty people who were making a robot to send to Mars. The robotic rover had to be sturdy enough to withstand the 119-million-mile journey and a potentially rough landing. It had to be "smart" enough to explore the cold, rough terrain of Mars and to send back information that could change our views of history and the future.*

In 1997, Donna Shirley cheered as cameras recorded the safe landing of the robotic rover. The rover, named Sojourner *for Sojourner Truth, used its tiny solar panels and flashlight batteries to shuttle around the red planet, collecting rocks and taking pictures of canyons and craters. Soil samples and rocks were brought back to Earth, where scientists continue to study them to answer such questions as: Was there life before life as we know it? Someday, can we fly to another planet and survive?*

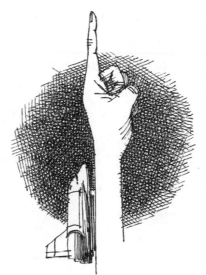

The Kennedy Space Center bustled as final plans were made to launch a shuttle that would carry the biggest piece of equipment ever taken into space. The *Chandra* X-ray Observatory was loaded onto a spacecraft that would be commanded, for the first time, by a woman. Lieutenant Colonel Eileen Collins welcomed crowds who'd come to see the launch. Sally Ride, who'd left NASA to teach college, was there, along with First Lady Hillary Clinton and her daughter, Chelsea, and over a dozen congresswomen. Most of the national women's soccer team, who'd made headlines by winning the World Cup earlier in that summer of 1999, jumped and cheered. NASA office workers waved signs that said, "You go, girl!"

Eileen Collins shook hands with women wearing WASP wings, whom she'd invited as her special guests. She hugged Jerrie Cobb, whose ponytail was more gray than blond now, and other women who'd hoped to be astronauts thirty-eight years before. The sky was turning dark. Eileen retreated to a room where she said goodbye to her husband and their daughter. Three-year-old Bridget touched her mother's orange space suit with curiosity, then nestled her head on her dad's shoulder. It was late, and she was sleepy.

Soon it was time for Eileen and the four crew members to climb into the van that would take them to the shuttle. Along the three-mile route, they waved at some of the workers who would support the flight from the ground, but had briefly left their desks to say good luck. Eileen Collins and the crew took the elevator up to the level where they'd board the shuttle. Technicians helped them into parachute harnesses and made sure their suits were airtight.

The five astronauts crawled through the hatch into *Columbia*. Eileen sat in the left-hand seat in front of the control panel. She knew its 1,300 switches well from practice on the simulator. She plugged in her communications cable and oxygen hose, then settled in for the usual two- or three-hour wait while final checks were done by people at Mission Control.

At T − 2 minutes before liftoff, Eileen switched on the oxygen flow. Firing rockets shook the shuttle. Their rumble and hiss was loud, but she could hear the countdown of seconds through her headphone. "Ten, nine, eight, seven."

Then there was a pause. At six seconds to liftoff, less than a second before the engines would ignite, the countdown stopped.

The activated systems were shut down. There might be a hydrogen leak, though possibly there was only a minor problem with the control panel. Eileen shrugged and managed a grin. After all, with over 2,300 miles of wire and six hundred circuit breakers in the shuttle, there was a lot that could go wrong.

The flight was postponed for forty-eight hours. That evening, rain fell over the bleachers, which weren't as crowded as they'd been two nights before. The First Lady, the congresswomen, and the soccer team had left for other scheduled events. But Eileen smiled at Jerrie Cobb and others of the Mercury 13 who'd waited half their lives to see a woman command a spacecraft. They had waited a few days more.

Again, Eileen kissed her husband and their sleepy daughter.

"Where are you going, Mommy?" Bridget asked.

"I'll be riding the shuttle." Eileen pointed to the silver spacecraft that glimmered in the rain and brilliant lights.

"Where will you go?"

"Up in the sky." Eileen raised her hand and watched her daughter's big eyes follow the motion, just as long ago she had watched her father's hand trace the sweep of gliders above a familiar hill.

"Can I come?" Bridget asked.

"Not tonight, honey, but sometime," Eileen said. "You can go anywhere you want."

Soon the astronauts drove to the shuttle, which had been rumbling through the day, its engines building the energy to lift the massive vehicle. Eileen glanced at the sky as lightning flashed. Then she checked her equipment and settled into her seat.

Five minutes before the shuttle was due to lift off, the launch was called off because the wind, rain, and lightning posed too great a risk.

Eileen climbed out of her space suit and returned to her husband and little girl. She would read *Goodnight Moon*, tuck Bridget into bed, and try to get some sleep. The launch was rescheduled for a few days later, but if everything didn't go well that time, Eileen might have to wait a few more months, since other missions were scheduled at the space center.

A few nights later, Eileen once again put on her space suit and said goodbye to her friends and family. She and the crew headed to the launchpad, where everything that had been checked and double-checked was checked again. Eileen settled into place and counted down. T − 4, T − 3, T − 2, T − 1.

At T − 0, the solid-fuel rocket boosters ignited. The bolts holding the shuttle to the platform exploded.

It was liftoff!

Eileen scanned the levers and gauges as the shuttle rose higher and flew faster. Nine seconds into the flight, she spoke into the microphone to Mission Control. The gauges indicated a fuel cell problem.

As *Columbia* soared over the Atlantic, Eileen kept her hands and voice calm, while she remembered practicing for emergency landings in Spain or Africa. Thirty seconds after she'd spoken, Mission Control radioed that there seemed to be a small problem with the electrical system, perhaps just a short circuit, which shouldn't affect the flight. All systems were go.

The shuttle kept flying over the ocean. Two minutes after liftoff, the force of gravity increased so that Eileen's arms felt almost too heavy to move. The solid-fuel rocket boosters were spent, and they dropped into the ocean, where they would be picked up by NASA staff waiting aboard ships. The shuttle began to shake less as it accelerated to twenty-five times the speed of sound.

Six minutes into the flight, checklists, flight manuals, and pencils began to float. Eileen smiled. It was great to be in zero gravity.

They cruised above Africa, then India and China. They soared over the Pacific. One wing covered Texas. Then they headed back over Florida, where Bridget would be sleeping, Eileen thought, tucked into bed with piles of stuffed animals beside her. Jerrie Cobb was probably still talking with her old friends, glancing at the sky from time to time.

Columbia circled the earth again, moving higher with each orbit. Around the world, some people slept while others woke up. Girls Eileen didn't know might be watching birds, the way Bessie Coleman used to do, or riding horses, as Amelia Earhart had done. Others, like Jackie Cochran, might be struggling to read and vowing to change their lives.

Eileen steered the shuttle far enough from Earth that the planet's light and dust couldn't interfere with the telescope's

vision. She and the crew slipped the *Chandra* X-ray Observatory into the black sky. Eileen flew away from the observatory, which was as tall as a building and weighed more than fifty thousand pounds. Then she turned back to watch it twisting in space. *Chandra* would point out stars no one had ever seen and planets where no one had yet landed. It might reveal secrets of the future in stars from the distant past. As it made X-ray images of our own Milky Way galaxy and of far-distant galaxies, it could show us new places to explore in a universe that was grander and greater than anyone had known.

Eileen Collins sat back in the commander's seat. Once one woman had sat here, others were bound to follow.

A NOTE FROM THE AUTHOR

In 1910 Blanche Stuart Scott was told that women couldn't fly. More than ten years later, Bessie Coleman learned that no flying school in the country would accept a black woman as a student. Amelia Earhart was told that women shouldn't cross oceans or continents in planes. Jackie Cochran and other women weren't allowed to fly military planes when World War II began. Jerrie Cobb was kept out of NASA's early space program because she was a woman.

Throughout almost a century of powered flight, women have refused to listen when told that they couldn't follow their hearts into the sky. Challenges remain. Today women make up about 25 percent of NASA and Air Force personnel, but only some of these women work as pilots. About one out of every twenty licensed aviators is a woman, and even fewer are commercial pilots. The heads of some airline companies worry that too many passengers would panic if they heard a woman's voice on the intercom, saying, "This is your pilot speaking."

Here I have compiled stories of women from different eras to show their common courage and love of flying while attitudes and aircraft changed. Since I covered so many years, I had to leave out the names and stories of many daring women. I focused on Americans and described only the highlights of the pilots' lives. Creating scenes with dialogue seemed the most efficient way to convey the spirit of the fliers, so I imagined dialogue and thoughts based on what the women wrote about themselves and what others said about them. All the magnificent accomplishments are real.

IMPORTANT YEARS IN WOMEN'S AVIATION HISTORY

1903: KATHARINE WRIGHT promises her brothers, Orville and Wilbur, to look after the house and their shop so they can take their flying machine to Kitty Hawk, North Carolina.

1910: BLANCHE STUART SCOTT becomes the first woman to pilot an airplane.

1911: HARRIET QUIMBY becomes the first woman to earn a pilot's license.

1912: HARRIET QUIMBY pilots a plane across the English Channel. Three months later, she dies when her plane crashes over Boston harbor.

1921: Flying in France, BESSIE COLEMAN becomes the first African American to earn a pilot's license.

1926: BESSIE COLEMAN dies after falling from a disabled plane.

1928: AMELIA EARHART becomes the first woman to cross the Atlantic Ocean in a plane.

1929: The first women's cross-country air race is held.

1929: The Ninety-Nines, an organization of women pilots that is still active, is formed.

1932: AMELIA EARHART becomes the first woman to pilot a plane across the Atlantic.

1932: After flying for two weeks, JACKIE COCHRAN earns a pilot's license.

1937: AMELIA EARHART disappears over the Pacific while attempting to fly around the world at the equator.

1941: JACKIE COCHRAN becomes the first woman to fly a warplane across the Atlantic. She joins British women aviators ferrying planes during World War II.

1942: JACKIE COCHRAN founds and directs the WASP, the Women's Airforce Service Pilots.

1944: WASP ANN BAUMGARTNER CARL becomes the first woman to pilot a jet aircraft.

1944: As World War II draws to an end, the WASP is disbanded.

1953: JACKIE COCHRAN becomes the first woman to break the sound barrier in a jet.

1961: JERRIE COBB and the Mercury 13 prepare to become astronauts.

1962: Women are banned from NASA's astronaut training program. The following year JERRIE COBB leaves for South America to fly food and medicine to remote villages.

1977: The WASP is given official military recognition.

1978: EILEEN COLLINS and several other women begin pilot training in the U.S. Air Force.

1978: Six women, including DR. SALLY RIDE and DR. SHANNON LU- CID, are accepted for astronaut training.

1983: SALLY RIDE becomes the first American woman in space.

1986: The space shuttle *Challenger* explodes, killing six astronauts and CHRISTA McAULIFFE, a teacher.

1990: EILEEN COLLINS is the first woman accepted for astronaut train- ing as a pilot.

1995: EILEEN COLLINS pilots a space shuttle.

1996: SHANNON LUCID spends 188 days on the Russian space station *Mir*, giving her a total of 223 days in space and setting a record for the longest time spent in space by any American in the twentieth cen- tury.

1999: EILEEN COLLINS becomes the first woman commander of a spacecraft.

IMPORTANT WOMEN IN AVIATION HISTORY

KATHARINE WRIGHT (1874–1929)

Wearing a long skirt tied around her ankles so it wouldn't blow in the wind, Katharine became one of the first women to ride in a powered aircraft. In *The Fun of It: Random Records of My Own Flying and of Women in Aviation*, Amelia Earhart quotes Orville Wright as saying, "When the world speaks of the Wrights, they should not forget our sister."

Orville depended upon Katharine so much that he was devasted when, at age fifty-two, she left home to marry Henry Haskell. Orville refused to attend the wedding and didn't speak to her until she was dying, about two years later, of pneumonia.

BLANCHE STUART SCOTT (1886?–1970)

Shortly after making a record-breaking automobile drive across the country, Blanche Stuart Scott became the first American woman to pilot a plane. In 1916, she retired from the air, saying, "In aviation there seems to be no place for the woman engineer, mechanic, or flier. Too often, people paid money to see me risk my neck, more as a freak—a woman freak pilot—than as a skilled flier. No more!"

HARRIET QUIMBY (1875–1912)

Harriet Quimby was a newspaper reporter who became the first woman to fly across the English Channel. She died in a plane crash eleven months after becoming the first woman to receive a pilot's license.

BESSIE COLEMAN (1892–1926)

The woman known as Queen Bess or Daring Bessie was the first person of color to earn a pilot's license, in 1921. Her death in a plane crash ended her dream of starting an aviation school for African Americans. It was finally fulfilled in 1942, when Willa Brown Chappell and her husband, Cornelius Coffey, opened the Coffey School of Aeronautics, where they trained many of the esteemed black pilots of World War II. Today Bessie Coleman's memory is honored every May 2, when pilots fly in formation over her grave in Chicago.

AMELIA EARHART (1897–1937)

In 1932, Amelia Earhart became the first woman to pilot a plane across the Atlantic Ocean. She was trying to set a record as the first person to fly around the earth at the equator when her plane disappeared over the Pacific.

RUTH NICHOLS (1901–60)

Ruth Nichols broke many speed and altitude records in the 1930s. In 1939, she founded an ambulance air service called Relief Wings, which eventually became part of the Civil Air Patrol. In 1949, while working for UNICEF, she became the first woman to circle the earth in a plane. She foresaw the possibilities of space flight years before NASA was founded, and wrote in her autobiography, *Wings for Life*, "Of one thing I am certain. When space ships take off, I shall be flying them, whether in my present bodily form or in another."

LOUISE THADEN (1905–79)

Louise Thaden won the first women's cross-country air race in 1929. She flew faster than any man or woman pilot to win the 1936 cross-country air race. She and her husband, Herb Thaden, raised two children and ran a business designing and building planes.

JACQUELINE COCHRAN (1906?–80)

Jackie Cochran's birth date was never recorded by the foster parents who raised her in various Florida mill towns. Jackie rose from poverty by mastering the beauty trade well enough to start her own cosmetics company. She learned how to pilot a plane in about two weeks, then went on to break more records than any other woman or man. During World War II, she founded the Women's Airforce Service Pilots, or WASP. She died not long after the WASP was finally given official military recognition, and was buried, as she'd requested, with the yellow-haired doll she had won as a child, given up, then gotten back.

ANN BAUMGARTNER CARL (1918–   )

As a WASP, Ann Baumgartner became the first woman to fly a jet aircraft. After the war she married, raised two children, and wrote many science articles and some books, including a memoir of her piloting experiences in World War II.

JERRIE (GERALDYN) COBB (1931–   )

Jerrie Cobb had spent about ten thousand hours in the air and broken many flight records when she became the first woman to test for astronaut training in 1960. Two years later, NASA officials declared that they had then no use for women astronauts. Jerrie left the country to fly food and medicine into remote regions of South America. In 1998, when seventy-seven-year-old John Glenn became the first senior citizen in space, a history teacher in California asked NASA why, if they thought it important to study the effects of space on an aging man, shouldn't they also send a senior woman into space? More than ten thousand schoolchildren and adults joined a grass-roots movement urging NASA to "do the right thing" and send Jerrie Cobb into space. She is still waiting, and still flying, carrying on the work she's done in the Amazon for over forty years.

SHANNON WELLS LUCID (1943–   )

Shannon Lucid holds the American record for the most time spent in space in the twentieth century. She continues to work for NASA, where she trains astronauts for work aboard the International Space Station. She hopes that she, too, will spend time on the space station, which was made possible by the efforts of sixteen countries.

EILEEN COLLINS (1956–   )

Lieutenant Colonel Eileen Collins was the first woman commander of a spacecraft.

DONNA SHIRLEY (1941–   )

Donna Shirley was the first woman to head a NASA program. She managed the Mars Exploration Program at the Jet Propulsion Laboratory in Pasadena, California. She supervised the building of a robotic rover, which, after landing on Mars in 1997, became the first vehicle to explore the surface of another planet.

BIBLIOGRAPHY

(Books noted with * were published for young readers.)

Bell, Elizabeth S. *Sisters of the Wind: Voices of Early Women Aviators.* Pasadena: Trilogy Books, 1994.

Boase, Wendy. *The Sky's the Limit: Women Pioneers in Aviation.* New York: Macmillan, 1979.

*Bredeson, Carmen. *Shannon Lucid: Space Ambassador.* Brookfield, Conn.: Millbrook Press, 1998.

*Briggs, Carole. *Women in Space.* Minneapolis: Lerner Publications, 1999.

*Buchanan, Doug. *Air and Space: Female Firsts in their Fields.* Philadelphia: Chelsea House Publishers, 1999.

Cadogan, Mary. *Women with Wings: Female Flyers in Fact and Fiction.* Chicago: Academy Chicago Publishers, 1993.

*Camp, Carole Ann. *Sally Ride: First American Woman in Space.* Springfield, N.J.: Enslow Publishing, 1997.

Carl, Ann B. *A Wasp Among Eagles.* Washington and London: Smithsonian Institution Press, 1999.

Cobb, Jerrie. *Jerrie Cobb, Solo Pilot.* Sun City Center, Fla.: Jerrie Cobb Foundation, 1997.

Cochran, Jackie. *The Stars at Noon.* Boston: Little, Brown, 1954.

Crouch, Tom D. *The Bishop's Boys: A Life of Wilbur and Orville Wright.* New York: W. W. Norton, 1989.

*Cummins, Julie. *Tomboy of the Air: Daredevil Pilot Blanche Stuart Scott.* New York: HarperCollins, 2001.

Earhart, Amelia. *The Fun of It: Random Records of My Own Flying and of Women in Aviation.* New York: Brewer, Warren and Putnam, 1932.

————. *Last Flight*. New York: Harcourt Brace, 1937.

————. *20 Hrs. 40 Mins.* New York: G. P. Putnam's Sons, 1928.

*Fox, Mary Virginia. *Women Astronauts Aboard the Shuttle.* New York: Julian Messner, 1984.

Harris, Sherwood. *The First to Fly: Aviation's Pioneer Days.* New York: Simon and Schuster, 1970.

Haynsworth, Leslie, and David Toomey. *Amelia Earhart's Daughters.* New York: William Morrow, 1998.

Hohler, Robert. *I Touch the Future: The Story of Christa McAuliffe.* New York: Random House, 1986.

Holden, Henry, and Lori Griffith. *Ladybirds II: The Continuing Story of Women in Aviation.* Mount Freedom, N.J.: Black Hawk Publishing, 1993.

Kessler, Lauren. *The Happy Bottom Riding Club: The Life and Times of Pancho Barnes.* New York: Random House, 2000.

Lomax, Judy. *Women of the Air.* New York: Dodd, Mead, 1987.

Lovell, Mary S. *The Sound of Wings: The Life of Amelia Earhart.* New York: St. Martin's Press, 1989.

Moolman, Valerie. *Women Aloft.* Alexandria, Va.: Time-Life Books, 1981.

Nichols, Ruth. *Wings for Life.* New York: Lippincott, 1957.

*O'Connor, Karen. *Sally Ride and the New Astronauts: Scientists in Space.* New York: Franklin Watts, 1983.

Peckham, Betty. *Women in Aviation.* New York: Thomas Nelson, 1945.

Rich, Doris. *A Biography of Amelia Earhart.* Washington, D.C., and London: Smithsonian Institution Press, 1989.

————. *The Magnificent Moisants.* Washington, D.C., and London: Smithsonian Institution Press, 1998.

————. *Queen Bess: Daredevil Aviator.* Washington, D.C., and London: Smithsonian Institution Press, 1993.

*Ride, Sally, with Susan Okie. *To Space and Back.* New York: Lothrop, Lee and Shepard, 1986.

Russo, Carolyn. *Women and Flight: Portraits of Contemporary Women Pilots.* Washington, D.C.: National Air and Space Museum, Smithsonian Institution, in association with Bulfinch Press, 1997.

Smith, Elinor. *Aviatrix*. New York and London: Harcourt Brace Jovanovich, 1981.

*Smith, Elizabeth Simpson. *Coming Out Right: The Story of Jacqueline Cochran, the First Woman Aviator to Break the Sound Barrier*. New York: Walker, 1991.

Strohfus, Elizabeth, as told to Cheryl J. Young. *Love at First Flight*. St. Cloud, Minn.: North Star Press, 1994.

Thaden, Louise. *High, Wide, and Frightened*. New York: Stackpole and Sons, 1938.

Verges, Marianne. *On Silver Wings: The Women Airforce Service Pilots of World War II*. New York: Ballantine Books, 1991.

*Yount, Lisa. *Women Aviators*. New York: Facts on File, 1995.

WEB SITES

THE NINETY-NINES
http://www.ninety-nines.org

SMITHSONIAN NATIONAL AIR AND SPACE MUSEUM: WOMEN
IN AVIATION AND SPACE HISTORY
http://www.nasm.si.edu/nasm/aero/women_aviators/womenavsp.htm

U.S. AIR FORCE MUSEUM
http://www.wpafb.af.mil/museum/history/wasp/wasp.htm

WOMEN IN AVIATION RESOURCE CENTER
http://www.women-in-aviation.com

WOMEN'S HISTORY: AVIATION
http://womenshistory.about.com

WOMEN OF NASA
http://quest.arc.nasa.gov/women/intro.html

INDEX